The ultimate guide to tricks, ramps, gear, setting up—and letting go!

SKATEBOARDING

written by

kevin wilkins

principal photography

by spike jonze

RUNNING PRESS
PHILADELPHIA, PENNSYLVANIA

dedicated to

cheryl

A FRIEDMAN GROUP BOOK

Copyright © 1994 by Michael Friedman Publishing Group, Inc.

9 8 7 6 5 4 3 2 1

Digit on the right indicates the number of this printing.

Library of Congress Cataloging-in-Publication Number 93-85515
ISBN 1-56138-377-5

SKATEBOARDING
The ultimate guide to tricks, ramps,
gear, setting up —and letting go!
was prepared and produced by
Michael Friedman Publishing Group, Inc.
15 West 26th Street
New York, New York 10010

Editor: Dana Rosen
Art Director: Jeff Batzli
Designers: Lori Thorn and Lizz Lambert
Photography Director: Christopher C. Bain
Photography Researcher: Ede Rothaus

Typeset by Élan Studio
Color separation by Bright Arts (Singapore) Pte. Ltd.
Printed and bound in China by Leefung-Asco Printers Ltd.

This book may be ordered by mail from the publisher.
Please add $2.50 for postage and handling.
But try your bookstore first.

Running Press Book Publishers
125 South Twenty-second Street
Philadelphia, Pennsylvania 19103-4399

TABLE OF CONTENTS

4

Max Evans doing a bump ollie over in-line skater.

INTRODUCTION

This is the introduction to a book. The intro is supposed to catch your attention, greet you, and give you a brief, but fact-filled prelude to the following pieces of pressed wood pulp and ink. It's also supposed to give you a tiny little taste of the rest of the book. So, here it goes:

This book is about skateboarding.

If you know anything about skateboarding, you'll probably like this short volume of photographic images and type. You might even like it if you don't skate. Then again, you might hate it. Either way, it's cool.

It was written and compiled to give a little insight— shallow, of course, because the only way to understand skating is to get on a board and stay there—of the pastime of literally thousands upon thousands of pre- and post-pubescent individuals. Skateboarding is still a toddler in the wide world of socially acceptable sports. But it's one of the more progressive activities a person can find—if one is looking to find progressive activities.

Anyway, just thumb through this book when you feel ready—you know, at your own speed. This is a high-stress world full of uncountable distractions. We wouldn't want to put any unnecessary pressure on you now, would we?

—kevin wilkins

STAND PIPE

Rodney Smith frozen for eternity in the painful position of a frontside wall-ride.
That has to hurt.

The Beginning

8

Frank Hirata executing a frontside noseslide on a handrail.

You can probably smell this from where you're sitting—Gary Harris guiding a quick noseslide accompanied by the long shadows of dusk.

In the beginning skateboards were garbage. But since they were all garbage, no one knew they were garbagy. Kind of like 8-track tapes—since there wasn't anything better to judge them by, no one knew how bad they were. As far as anyone was concerned, the first skateboards were state of the art.

Some people believe that the first skateboarder was a surfer who, one day when the waves were not calling, went into a motion-deprived craziness, ripped apart the nearest pair of roller skates, and nailed them to a two-by-four. Rolling on this is supposed to have suppressed his wave-starved appetite. More surfers took up the boards and the term sidewalk surfing was coined, or so legend has it.

Others claim skateboards came from somewhere other than the United States' West Coast. They'll swear it originated in the Midwest, Northeast, South, or almost anywhere else that's landlocked. They believe that the skateboard developed from a push scooter—which is very similar to the ripped-apart-skate-and-two-by-four idea, but has the addition of a wooden crate as a sort of handle. And unlike the West Coast's surf influence, the scooter and skateboard combo didn't develop from any particular activity, but from the lack of one. Boredom. There's probably some catchy old saying to insert here about boredom breeding great ideas and inventions, but nothing really comes to mind. Maybe you're bored enough to come up with one yourself.

Oh, hey, the newest and neatest idea regarding the birth of the skateboard has it as the result of a slow, but profitable, evolution from the pioneer wagons:

"The skateboard is a direct descendant of the wagon. The bicycle is its closest relative. Before the beginning of the nineteenth century, wagons were used primarily for transportation, most notably the Conestoga wagon, which symbolized the move

westward in the mid-1800s. The advent of the bicycle in the early 1800s brought about a change in people's outlooks on wheeled objects: They saw them as something other than transportation for the first time.

During the twentieth century, wagons evolved from a major source of transportation to a popular toy for small children. A scaled-down wagon without the sides and with the handle fixed vertically is a scooter. And even simpler, a scooter without the handle is a skateboard."

—From "A View Without A Room," by Britt Parrott, TransWorld Skateboarding Magazine, October 1989

Anyway, no one really knows when the first skateboard was actually called a skateboard, who called it that, and where he or she lived. And that's just fine. At least it's not written in some history book as being discovered by Christopher Columbus or something like that.

As anyone who has ridden one of those frustrating dinosaurs can attest, it's easy to see why the first wave of skateboarding was short-lived. The fun factor was low and so was the progression of the aforementioned sidewalk surfers.

Ron Kniqqe bump to bump double kickflip.

Ray Underhill blowing a melanchollie drifter under the billowing exhaust of yet another Southern California brush fire.

Evolution of
Skateboards

In the 1970s, skateboarding became fashionable again, partly because of the investment opportunities available to property owners who could open the world's newest money-maker— skateboard parks. The parks meant more places to skate. More places to skate meant more people skating. More people skating meant more equipment being sold. More equipment being sold meant more equipment needed to be made. It was beautiful. Capitalism at its peak of obscenity. Get rich quick and then get out quicker.

Fortunately, the skateboarding boom of the 1970s was large enough and lasted long enough that some bona fide skate businesses were established. These were, for the most part, the companies who developed and offered quality skate products and pushed for the advancement of skateboarding as a sport. Many of these are still in existence and thriving today. Enough companies like Tracker, Powell Peralta, Z, Santa Cruz, Gullwing, and others concentrated on making a good product and supported skateboarding as a real sport — not just the latest wave of faddish money-making — so that skateboarding was able to get a foothold for staying alive. After the fad wore off, there was a small but devoted group of hardcore skateboarders. They not only worked to keep the skating business alive, but kept skating because it was a fun, progressive new sport.

The sharp wane in skateboarding's popularity in the early 1980s had a lot to do with the near extinction of skateparks. Lack of interest due to poor design, high admission fees, and insurance problems brought a quick death to the era of the concrete skateboard park. Although some concrete parks managed to escape

This is Saecha Clarke just moments after ollieing into this 50-50.
Moments later, she was doing something else.

the steel blade of the bulldozer, skateboarders were slowly but surely shoved out of their habitat.

But by this time, the skateboarding community had become strong. They quickly learned that they could make skateboarding whatever they wanted it to be. Backyard ramps were built in greater numbers and the street became more intensively ridden. It wasn't really the death of skateboarding—actually more of a rebirth on the most grass-roots level. Skateboarders realized that even though the big companies were failing and the parks were closing, skateboarding was still going strong. Instead of going strong in view of everybody and their mother, it found strength underground. Instead of following a path that was set up for them, the skaters took their little activity and made it a legitimate thing—even if it was only within their own realm. Now skateboarding has its own defense system—it's goof proof. If bad things are happening with skateboarding (as did in the past, and will surely happen in the future), skateboarding just kicks back for a while and all that extra lame weight (quick-buck seekers, big-time promoters, etc.) comes right off. It's that easy. Some might say, "The reason the weight comes off that easy is because skateboarding is starving itself. If it doesn't eat, it's sure to die." And skateboarding says, "Well, that's a chance I gotta take."

In 1983 the first pro-am streetstyle contest took place, laying the foundation for modern street skating. Small backyard contests and eventually contest series like M.E.S.S. (Mid Eastern Skateboard Series) and M.A.R.S. (Midwest Amateur Ramp Series) were organized in the United States and run by skaters. Skaters in other countries grouped together. A close-knit network of small photocopied magazines called 'zines kept skaters around the world clued in to what was going on in other areas. Things were starting to look good again by 1985, with the National Skateboard Association going strong and regular amateur and pro contests taking place. People started talking of the sport getting huge—Olympics and stuff like that. Skateboarders just kept skateboarding. They'd seen and heard big-money talk before and knew that in the long run such flash would make little difference. They'd still be skating and there would still be skateboarders no matter how huge, or miniscule, skateboarding promotion got.

Ortho Stevens charging a hard frontside grind at the AIDS Bowl.

The

Importance of the Sport Today

Ron Chatman nose manualing into the night.

Skateboarding today, although becoming more and more mainstream, offers something very unique to anyone wanting to become involved. Skateboarding is an individual sport. Anyone can do it, and you don't need other people to participate in the activity, although other people can make it more interesting. There are no rule books, no coaches, no set arenas, no nothing—just you and your skateboard. Step outside your house and get involved.

The individualism and physical challenge of skateboarding attract people of all ages, races, and backgrounds. Skateboarding holds no prejudices. In skateboarding you are free to do as you please and express yourself in any way, shape, or form. There is no right or wrong way to skateboard. Don't let anyone tell you there is.

"There you are, street skating in the downtown area with a couple of your closest skate buddies, when all of a sudden you are confronted by two older skaters who seem to think that your style of skating just isn't right. One opens his mouth, and out comes, 'Why are you trying all that board-flip, melanchollie, impossible crap?' And the other continues with, 'I bet you can't even slappy that curb frontside.'

How many times have you heard that sort of remark? Probably too many. If your response is that you can't do a slappy or have never seen anyone do one—don't feel bad, because you're not alone. Don't let their narrow view of skateboarding get in the way of progressing in the manner that you want. It's not your fault that you weren't skating when the slappy was the "popular" trick. This is the 90s, and the basics are on a whole different level than they were five years ago. So it's okay to learn an ollie impossible before a slappy.

Still, there are some mandatory fundamentals you must conquer, such as: standing on your skateboard and riding down a hill without falling off, turning, backside and frontside kickturns, and dropping into a ramp. Then you can think about learning maneuvers that take a little more skill: ollies, shove-its, 50-50s, and so on. Hopefully, you'll skate long enough—and with an open mind—to be able to do every trick you see, unlike the sort of guy that closes his mind to new and different types of skating."

—From "Speak," by Dave Swift, TransWorld Skateboarding Magazine, October 1989

The Virtues of Selfishness

Skateboarding attracts the people of our community who feel they don't need to adhere to any preset track. They do what they do because it's what they want. This might seem like an ultimately selfish attitude—progressing in an activity for one's own personal reasons, and not for the good of some cause, or the cause of some greater good. In fact, it *is* selfish. But this act of being selfish is not taking place in order to take power over something or to gain ground over someone. It is a sort of personal selfishness. Progressing simply because you can progress. Challenging one's own limits. Striving for that feeling you can only get when you are one with your skateboard—that feeling when it's second nature to roll, lean, turn, and unweight at just the right time. It's kind of hard to explain, but you'll know it when you feel it. Oh, by the way, this feeling can be experienced by anyone who steps on a skateboard— from the first-day beginner to the ten-year veteran. So don't hold

Steve Berra knows that riding the opposite direction you're used to is difficult. Switch-stance 360 kickflip.

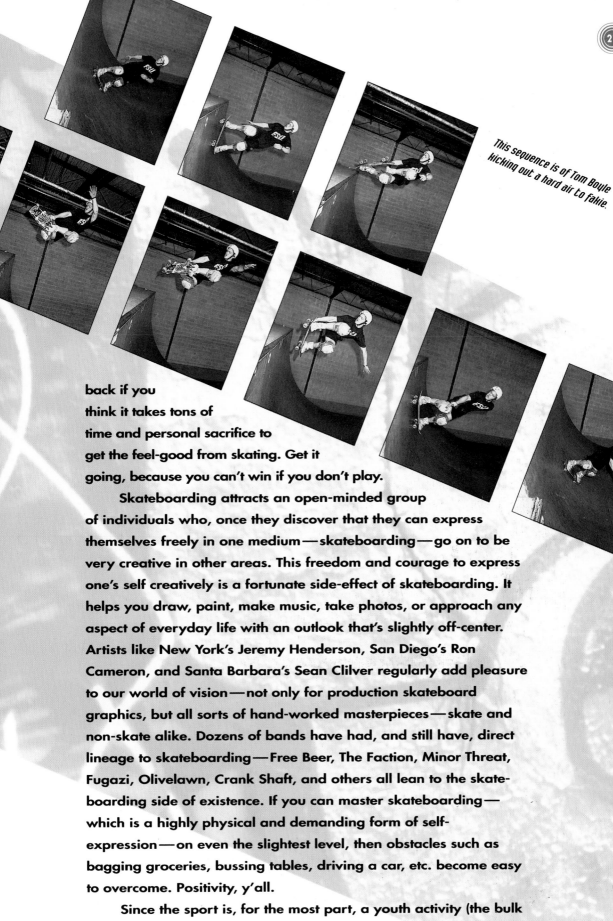

This sequence is of Tom Boyle kicking out a hard air to fakie.

back if you think it takes tons of time and personal sacrifice to get the feel-good from skating. Get it going, because you can't win if you don't play.

Skateboarding attracts an open-minded group of individuals who, once they discover that they can express themselves freely in one medium—skateboarding—go on to be very creative in other areas. This freedom and courage to express one's self creatively is a fortunate side-effect of skateboarding. It helps you draw, paint, make music, take photos, or approach any aspect of everyday life with an outlook that's slightly off-center. Artists like New York's Jeremy Henderson, San Diego's Ron Cameron, and Santa Barbara's Sean Clilver regularly add pleasure to our world of vision—not only for production skateboard graphics, but all sorts of hand-worked masterpieces—skate and non-skate alike. Dozens of bands have had, and still have, direct lineage to skateboarding—Free Beer, The Faction, Minor Threat, Fugazi, Olivelawn, Crank Shaft, and others all lean to the skate-boarding side of existence. If you can master skateboarding—which is a highly physical and demanding form of self-expression—on even the slightest level, then obstacles such as bagging groceries, bussing tables, driving a car, etc. become easy to overcome. Positivity, y'all.

Since the sport is, for the most part, a youth activity (the bulk of skaters being eighteen and under), it instills courage, individuality,

and freedom of expression early in life. And the earlier you find out that you are an okay person without needing to cling to the world's preset role models for identity, the easier it becomes to cope with life's little challenges.

In skateboarding, there is little room for ego tripping, although as in any facet of life, it does exist. Why bother? An egotistical point of view is only going to hold you down. If your way of doing things is seen by you as being superior, how are you going to be able to see the ideas of others that might help you live a fuller life? Huh? Deep, man, real deep.

Even though skateboarders are individuals, skateboarding bridges all gaps and brings people together from every race, creed, and country. Few things speak such a universal language. You can go anywhere in the world and if you have a skateboard, you can hook up with any other skateboarder and click instantly. And why shouldn't you? Without any words being spoken, skateboarders can exchange ideas through their love of skateboarding. Anyone who rides a skateboard is considered kin. The concept of there being no right or wrong way to skateboard spreads out and becomes the concept of there being no right or wrong outlook regarding any aspect of life. And the sooner we learn to accept others as human beings who have the right to think any way they want, the sooner we will be able to stop things like war, prejudice,

Jeremy Klein kicking one-foot over an A.W.O.L. shopping cart.

You can see that these images are of Todd Congelliere pumping, grabbing, and releasing a very solid frontside air.

and hate. Any vehicle that can deliver that message is important and legitimate.

    Skateboarding has also done a complete turn around in the world of influence. In the beginning, it was said that skateboarding got many of its moves from its supposed mother, surfing. Well, take that and turn it 360. Today, skateboarding is a major influence on surfing. Now there are surfers popping airs out of waves and grabbing a rail here or there. Yes, turnabout is fair play. Snowboarding also owes most of its moves and terminology to skateboarding. Even tricks invented by and named after pro skateboarders enjoy a softer alternative lifestyle in the world of snowboarding. Nowadays, Caballerials, half Cabs, Miller flips, Elgerials, Phillips 76, and McTwist's are all being executed on the snow. So, if the importance of a sport can be measured by its influence, skateboarding is possibly the most important sport in all of history.

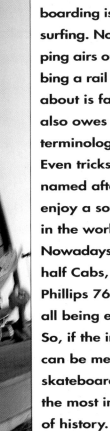

If you look really close at this photo of Ray Barbee,
you can see the tiny shards of paint and concrete being left in the wake of his nose grind.

Alex Morrison tail tapping in one
of Vancouver, B.C.'s public skateparks.

All-
Terrain Vehicle

The terrain of skateboarding is anywhere. Is that vague enough for you?
Well, good. Skateboarding offers the freedom of movement that hardly any
other activity can equal: the freedom to go wherever a skateboard will roll.
That's mind-boggling amounts of freedom. Parking lots, sidewalks, school
yards, driveways, streets, dirt, grass, handrails, stairs, pools, ramps, and so
on. But for the sake of space we'll divide skateboarding's terrain into three
groups: ramps, street, and pools.

Ramps

Do you know what a ramp is? No? Well, think of an onramp to a freeway or a
handicapped ramp. Those are ramps. The first ramps were most likely plywood
leaned up against something—a board set on a brick. But that was then and
this is now, so get those slanted-wood ideas out of your head. Are they out of
there? Okay, now put this in: *transitions*. Hungry for more? Read on.

VERTICAL

Today's vertical terrain is the descendant of yesterday's skateparks, which
were the descendants of backyard pools. Quite a chain, isn't it? And one with
strong links. If any of the three are found today, they are no doubt being
sessioned regularly. Vert won't go in and out of style—it's just another place
to ride. The ideal vertical ramp stands somewhere between ten and twelve
feet tall (3.0-3.6 m) and has one to two feet of vert (30-60 cm), the mid-range
being eleven feet (3.3 m) in the height department and one and a half feet
(45 cm) in the vertical department. Here's the explanation for those of you less
knowledgeable: The transition of a ramp is the curved part. It is measured by
how tall it is. On a ramp with nine-and-a-half-foot transitions (2.85 m), the
curved part will be nine and a half feet tall. This can then be topped with
vertical. Vertical means straight up and down. A foot and a half (45 cm) of
vertical would make our ramp eleven feet tall (3.3 m). Width and flat bottom
are up to you, but there are some loose standards that can make your ramp a
whole lot better. Flat bottom is the flat part that is in between the two curved
parts. Sixteen feet (4.8 m) is pretty standard, and you can vary this one or

two feet (30-60 cm) and still be pretty safe. Any more and you feel like you are waiting for the next wall; any less and it comes up way too quickly. But, you can get used to anything.

On a ramp of this height, you should probably stay over twenty-four feet (7.2 m) of width—wider if possible. But if you are limited by space you can do whatever you want. Any ramp will be fun if it's built correctly. More on miniramps and small structures later.

If you want to include a channel, extensions, escalators, or anything of that sort, you should be sure your ramp

Chris Miller has been sentenced to stall this Smith-vert until the end of time in the pages of this book.

is wider than thirty-six feet (10.8 m). Those little lip mutations take away from the flat wall that you need in order to grind, ride, and move around. A channel in the way will get old after a while. An extension will, too. Make sure there's plenty of opposing flat wall. If you want all that other stuff, at least do it over a twenty-four-foot (7.2 m) marker.

Channels add a new twist to any trick. If you think you can do it well, do it over the channel. Extensions should always come in pairs and oppose each other. If you only have one, it becomes a crutch and a hindrance. Depending on which way you stand, you can only do certain tricks on it. A pair is much better. Escalators are cool. They are angled portions of a ramp that connect a regular-height flat wall with an extension. This enables you to have extensions and a few feet more of grindable lip.

Today's ramp is topped with coping, which means curved edge. Steel pipe coping is most common—about one and a half to two inches (4-5 cm) in diameter. Concrete pool coping, aluminum pipe, PVC, and wood can also be used, but with mixed results.

PVC plastic pipe is used for plumbing or electrical work. It's the easiest coping to get a hold of, but it's too slick and breaks very easily.

Wood is lame and should never be used. Not only will it be hard to grind, but people will think you're a dope.

Aluminum is lame, too. It gets dented and sticky after continuous use and then people start to wax it. This makes the coping slick and uncontrollable. Wax is then tracked onto the surface of the ramp which makes it slick and dangerous.

Concrete pool coping is cool. It's called pool coping because it's the same material that makes the round lip around lots of pools. It makes beautiful noises when you grind it and makes you feel tough. It's hard to get a hold of, but the reward of nice, hard concrete coping is worth any difficulty.

MINIRAMPS

Miniramps are just that—small-sized ramps. They don't have vert. Someone's answer to the sheer height of vertical, miniramps became popular in the late 1980s and currently enjoy a healthy existence on our planet. The most common species of

Primarily thought of as a street skater, Jason Lee shrugs all labels aside as he powers through this ally-oop nose grind atop twelve feet [4m] of wooden transition.

miniramp is the five-to-six-foot-high (1.5-1.8 m), eight-to-sixteen-foot-wide (2.4-4.8 m) variety with eight-to-eight-and-a-half-foot (2.4-2.5 m) transitions. The transition-to-height ratio is the most crucial factor in a good miniramp. Too tight and you'll be bummed. Too mellow and you'll be bummed, too. It might sound hard—that's because it is. Many skateboarders have spent hours building ramps, and because of not enough planning beforehand, they ended up with a useless pile of wood and nails. Don't blow it.

Street

The street is the most accessible terrain in all of skateboarding. Look outside, what do you see? The street. That doesn't just mean the concrete designated as pathways for cars and other fuel-powered forms of transportation. In skateboarding the street is defined as anywhere other than ramps. Anywhere that can be ridden. Anything that can be ridden. Curbs, stairs, embankments, ditches, handrails, planters, benches, cracks in the sidewalk—anything. Unfortunately, usually these anythings are owned or policed by someone who doesn't want skateboards ridden on them. Skateboards and their users are not wanted or widely accepted in our communities. People think they're too loud, too dirty, too out of control, too rebellious, and too stupid.

Nighttime is the right time. Places of business are usually closed and their proprietors are at home in front of the television. This is *your* prime time. Take advantage of the sparse nighttime population to skate places that are normally crowded or policed by day. Grocery stores, malls, banks, restaurants, school grounds, and college campuses all have a large and hostile population during the day, but at night everyone moves their cars and carcasses so you can have more personal space. You don't

Big things come in little packages. Such is the case here as Chris Branagh kicks this fat backside ollie one-foot off your average driveway curb.

even have to ask them, everyone just leaves around five o'clock. Hurray for you.

Street is also, by far, the fastest developing and most influential branch of skateboarding. The rate of progression and development of new, seriously technical tricks is staggering. And since street is the most highly accessible type of skating, it's safe to say that its progression is nowhere near the end.

Pools

Pools are by far the rarest form of skating terrain. To find an empty pool, skate it, and not get caught is one of the purest forms of skateboarding. You truly adapt to your environment.

Carefully evaluate the scene before sessioning. Is the pool drained? Is the house vacant? Neighbors? Is the pool hidden from view? Try a quick session first, just to get a taste of the pool. Tight transitions are usually the norm, but occasionally a giant is found and ridden for a while until it's discovered by a non-skater and filled or bulldozed. To conquer a pool by means of a short session is overwhelming. Carving frontside, backside, and may-be doing a grind can make you feel larger than life.

If there is the slightest bit of concrete around, Tom Groholski will be riding it.

Frank Hirata performs the frontside 180 to backward front truck grind to gazelle off the well-worn Big Bear curb in Oceanside, California.

The Tricks

Skaters Do

Text and Photos by Dave Swift, TransWorld Skateboarding Magazine

Now that you're pretty far into this book about skateboarding, you're probably getting pretty stoked right now and want to learn some new tricks.
And what better way to learn than to look at sequences of some of today's
best professional and amateur skateboarders doing the most modern and
technical tricks around—and with some words of explanation to boot?

Hopefully you already are familiar with some of the basics, like
riding in a straight line, down a hill, tick-tacking, etc. Also, it's important to
know which way you stand on a skateboard: If your right foot is forward
then you are called a goofy footer. If you are one of those skaters whose
left foot is at the front of the board, than you are known as a regular
footer. Your stance should come naturally—you'll know which you are
the first time you walk up to a skateboard and stand on it.

Another important aspect of skateboarding that doesn't often get
talked about is the direction you are turning at any given time. The two
directions are called frontside and backside. If you are a goofy footer,
frontside is when you turn to the right and backside is anytime you turn to
the left (the opposite is true for regular footers). A fakie is when you are
riding backward (in modern street skating this is often called opposite-
footed because the foot that is forward on the board is the opposite of
your regular stance).

The Ollie

(GAPS, BUMPS, RAMPS, HANDRAILS, CURBS, BENCHES, BANKS)

The first trick a beginning skater wants to learn, with the exception of rolling
down the street and maintaining one's balance, is the ollie, or no-handed
air. The ollie was pioneered by then-unknown and later Powell-Peralta
professional skateboarder Alan Gelfand of Florida (the name "Ollie" was
Alan's nickname). The ollie is in one way or another incorporated into
every modern skateboarding trick.

BASIC FLATGROUND OLLIE

1. Go out and find a flat area of cement (schoolyards and vacant parking lots are always good), take a couple of pushes, and ride in a straight line with the back foot on the tail and the front foot about midway between the trucks.
2. Bend down and then quickly snap upward with your front foot and snap the tail as though you are jumping up into the air. The front of the board will get almost vertical. At this moment, suck the back foot up into the body and at the same time push downward on the nose with the front foot until the board is level or the nose is pointing slightly downward.
3. Now that you can get the board off the ground, try ollieing up curbs, over a friend's skateboard, or over whatever you can find. The ollie takes lots of practice and the more a skater practices, the higher he or she will be able to do them.

VARIATIONS: Every trick is a variation of the ollie.

FRONTSIDE 180 OLLIE

1. Once you have regular ollies wired, this will probably be the next maneuver you will want to learn.
2. Ride straight toward the curb, bench, rail, or whatever you intend to ollie over.
3. When you are within range, pop a regular ollie but rotate your shoulders 180 degrees in the frontside direction, and the lower half of your body should follow.
4. Land backward; you'll probably end up landing on your front wheels at first, but just keep practicing and you'll get it right really quick.

VARIATIONS: Backside 180 ollie, backside half-Cab (fakie 180), frontside half-Cab.

BACKSIDE 360 OLLIE

1. Before learning the backside 360, you first need to master backside 180s off curbs or on flat ground.
2. Ride straight toward the edge of the curb at the speed you feel comfortable.
3. As you near the edge, bend down, start rotating your body backside, and do an ollie.

4. At first you'll probably end up doing 270s, but keep trying and you should end up doing a complete 360.

5. Your front foot will probably come off the nose a little at first, but don't worry because some of your friends will probably think you did it on purpose.

VARIATIONS: Frontside 360 ollie, opposite-footed 360 ollie, Caballerial, frontside Caballerial.

Kickflip

(GAPS, BUMPS, RAMPS, HANDRAILS, CURBS, BENCHES, BANKS)

The kickflip has been around since the mid-seventies, but the original version was quite different from what is performed today by nearly every skateboarder in the world. In its early incarnation, the kickflip was performed by flatland freestylers who stood with their feet parallel in the middle of the board and used the arches of their feet to flip the board. Some ten years later (around 1985 or 1986) top street skaters such as Mark Gonzales and Natas Kaupus developed the modern version for more practical street use.

BASIC KICKFLIP

1. Before learning how to do kickflips while rolling, learn them while stationary by placing the rear wheels of your board in a sidewalk crack.

2. Stand with your back foot near the end of the tail, and place the toes of your front foot on the outside rail about four or five inches (10 or 13cm) behind the front truck bolts.

Jeremy Klein executes the backside 360 ollie.

3. Bend down and then quickly snap upward with your front foot as though you are jumping up into the air (just as you would for an ollie).

4. As soon as you snap the board, kick down and forward on the rail with your front foot, thus making the board do a single flip. This step will take a lot of practice (and patience) before the board starts flipping right. Don't forget to stay directly over the top of the board.

5. Once the board has done a complete flip, land on it. Get kickflips wired in the stationary position and then start trying them while you are moving.

KICKFLIP TO 50-50 GRIND TO SHOVE-IT OFF

1. Ride at a comfortable speed toward the curb.

2. When you are about two feet (0.6m) away from the curb, do an ollie kickflip and aim it so that you land in a 50-50 grind (grinding on both the front and back axle) on the edge of the curb.

3. When you come to the end of the curb, do a backside shove-it (push to your backside with your rear foot while unweighting and lifting upward with your front foot) and the whole time stay directly above your board.

4. Land both feet on the top of the board.

VARIATIONS: Double kickflip, 360 kickflip, kickflip to noseslide, half-cab kickflip, frontside 180 kickflip, hard-flip (frontside shove-it kickflip).

The Backfoot Flip

(GAPS, BUMPS, RAMPS, HANDRAILS, BANKS, CURBS, STEPS)

In the last year or so, skaters have adopted many different types of board flips, and the backfoot flip seems to be one of the most popular. Basically, the backfoot flip is just a kickflip using the back foot instead of the front. You're probably thinking, "Hey, that sounds easy," but when you try it you'll find out that a backfoot flip can be pretty tough, especially if you've already learned the basic kickflip. But just like most of today's modern skateboard tricks, the backfoot flip just takes a lot of practice.

BACKFOOT FLIP 180 TO NOSE DRIVE REVERT

1. Ride up whatever it is you are going to do this trick on and pop an ollie.

2. Once the board is off the ground, start rotating your body backside and at the same time lift your front foot off the nose and kick down with your back foot so that the board does a flip.

3. Land on the board with most of your weight forward so that your back wheels never touch the ground and rotate another 180 degrees (nose drive revert) and roll away fakie.

VARIATIONS: Backside 180 late backfoot flip, backfoot heelflip, backfoot flip to railslide, Caballerial backfoot flip (vert ramps), fakie ollie backfoot flip (ramps).

Heelflip

(GAPS, BUMPS, RAMPS, HANDRAILS, CURBS, BENCHES, BANKS)

The heelflip has gained a lot of popularity within the skate world in the last few years. We're not really sure who the pioneers of this variation of the kickflip are, but you can put money down that Mark Gonzales, Natas Kaupus, and Rodney Mullen had something to do with it.

BASIC HEELFLIP

1. Once again, you might have better luck if you learn heelflips in the stationary mode by putting your back wheels in a sidewalk or other crack.

2. Put your back foot near the end of the tail and set your front foot about five inches (13cm) behind the front truck bolts with your toes hanging slightly over the inside rail.

3. Bend down and then quickly snap upward with your front foot, as though you are jumping up into the air (just like an ollie).

4. At this point you want to push your front foot down and forward very quickly, which should make the board flip. Once again, this will take lots of practice but in the end it will be worth it.

5. Stay directly over the board as it flips and land on it once it has completely rotated.

6. Now try them as you are rolling.

FRONTSIDE VARIAL (SHOVE-IT) HEELFLIP

1. Try this trick on flat ground before doing it off stairs or gaps.

2. Ride straight with the toes of your front foot hanging off the inside or frontside rail and your back foot's heel hanging off the outside or backside of the tail.

Jeff Toland executes the frontside varial heelflip.

3. Shove the board toward frontside with your rear foot while at the same time going through the motions of a heelflip with your front foot (see the step-by-step for a regular heelflip).

4. Now that the board is spinning and flipping, you'll want to suck your legs up toward your body until the board has done a complete flip and 180 shove-it.

5. Now all you need to do is land both feet on the ground and ride away.

VARIATIONS: Frontside half-Cab heelflip, backside 180 heelflip, opposite-footed heelflip, nollie heelflip, double heelflip, heelflip to indy grab (ramps).

Impossible

(GAPS, CURBS, HANDRAILS, BUMPS, BANKS, BENCHES, STAIRS)

The impossible is a strange flip trick because the board doesn't flip, but rotates 360 around the front or back foot quickly. Although the impossible isn't all too popular at the moment, a few years ago it was *the* trick to do.

BACK FOOT IMPOSSIBLE

1. Roll forward as though you are going to do a standard backside shove-it but hang your front off the side of the board.

2. Now lift your front foot off the board and swing it to the side (so it is out of the way), while at the same time scooping the tail with your back foot.

3. If you've scooped correctly, the board should be wrapping around your back foot.

4. Once the board has done a full rotation (360 degress), let it land on the ground (your back foot should be somewhere near the at this point) and quickly put your front foot back on the board.

VARIATIONS: Front foot impossible, impossible to railside, impossible to noseslide, tail-grab impossible, impossible to nose tap to fakie (ramp).

Nollie

(GAPS, BUMPS, RAMPS, HANDRAILS, STAIRS, BENCHES, CURBS, BANKS)

The nollie was invented by Natas Kaupus in the mid-eighties and is basically just an ollie off the nose.

1. Ride with your front foot on the nose and your trailing foot about five inches (13cm) in front of the back truck bolts.
2. Bend and push downward with your front foot while at the same time bringing your back leg up toward your torso in a snapping motion similar to an ollie.
3. When the board gets vertical, lift upward with your front foot until the board is horizontal to the ground.
4. Land just as you would for an ollie.

VARIATIONS: Backside and frontside nollie 180, nollie kickflip and heelflip, nollie to noseslide, nollie to 5-0 (frontside or backside), nollie to 5-0 grind to backward grind.

Railslide

(CURBS, RAILS, BENCHES, RAMPS, POOLS)

The railslide (both backside and frontside) was developed in concrete skateparks and on ramps (vertical, rock 'n' roll slide) and soon after was adapted by street skaters when curbs and handrails were discovered as skateable objects.

BACKSIDE RAILSLIDE

1. Ride (backside) toward the bench, handrail, curb, or whatever you want to slide parallel or at a slight angle.
2. When you are near enough to the obstacle, ollie up onto it, landing with the bottom of your board (between the trucks) on its surface.
3. Keep most of your weight centered directly over the board but lean back slightly so that you slide.
4. Slide as far as you can, and when you want to come off put more of your weight on the tail and turn 45 degrees.
5. Land all four wheels on the ground and ride off.

FRONTSIDE RAILSLIDE

The frontside railslide is pretty much the same as the backside variation except that you approach the bench, handrail, or curb, etc. frontside. Balancing a frontside railslide will seem to be more difficult than balancing a backside, but like most skateboard tricks, the more you practice the easier it will become.

BACKSIDE RAILSLIDE TO BACKWARD FRONT TRUCK GRIND

1. Approach the curb or bench with enough speed to slide the length of it.
2. Ollie up onto the curb and start backside boardsliding.
3. At some point you want to push the tail of your board forward and up while at the same time putting all of your weight on the nose, until you feel the front truck begin to grind.
4. When you are near the end of the curb, shift your weight to the tail and turn forty-five degrees until you are facing forward once again.
5. Land all four wheels at the same time and then go on to other variations.

VARIATIONS: Railslide to noseslide, railslide to backward grind, 5-0 grind to railslide, railslide to noseblunt slide transfer.

Lipslide

The lipslide was born and bred back in the seventies by early practitioners of ditches and cement skateparks. In the mid- to late eighties lipslides—frontside, backside, fakie, etc.—became standard moves on ramps and curbs everywhere.

LIPSLIDE REVERT

1. The first type of lipslide you will want to try is the frontside version because it tends to be easier than the others.
2. Ride frontside toward the curb at about a forty-five-degree angle.
3. When you are about two feet (0.6m) away do a frontside 180 ollie, guiding the board so that the area between the trucks lands on the surface of the curb.
4. Stay on top of your board but lean back enough so that you still slide along the top of the curb.
5. When you feel your board slow down (but are still moving laterally along the top of the curb), lean forward on your front foot and lift up slightly on your rear foot. This action will get you off the curb.
6. When you know that the rear wheels have cleared the lip, keep turning until you are heading down the wall backward (revert).

VARIATIONS: Lipslide to Smith grind, lipslide to noseblunt slide, lipslide to tailslide, backside lipslide, frontside or backside lipslide to overturned grind, 5-0 grind to lipslide.

Noseslide

Although this trick has been around for a few years, it has only recently become one of the most popular tricks done on the streets and ramps.

BASIC BACKSIDE NOSESLIDE

1. Ride backside and at a slight angle toward the bench you wish to noseslide.
2. When you are about two to three feet (0.6 to 1m) away, do a ninety-degree frontside ollie, eyeing the edge of the bench the whole time.
3. With your front foot up near the front of the nose, push it into the edge of the bench until you feel your front truck against it.
4. Get on top of your board and the bench but lean back enough so that you are sliding.
5. When you feel yourself begin to slow down, put most of your weight on your tail and turn your shoulders (the board should follow) ninety degrees backside.
6. Land all four wheels at the same time.

VARIATIONS: Frontside noseslide, half-cab noseslide, opposite-footed noseslide, fakie to backward nosegrind to noseslide, noseslide to noseblunt slide transfer (double-sided curbs), frontside noseslide to backside shove-it off, frontside noseslide to backward nose-grind to fakie.

FRONTSIDE NOSESLIDE TO BACKSIDE SHOVE-IT

1. Ride at an angle toward the bench, railing, or planter with an average amount of speed.
2. Ollie up and turn your board forty-five degrees in the frontside direction.
3. Push forward with your front foot until the nose of your board is sliding on the surface of the obstacle you are riding.
4. When you are near the end of the

Paulo Diaz executing a handrail noseslide.

obstacle, push forward on the tail of your board with your back foot while at the same time unweighting your front foot (backside shove-it) and staying directly above the board.

5. Land on the board and roll away.

FRONTSIDE NOSESLIDE TO BACKWARD FRONT TRUCK GRIND TO FAKIE

1. To do this trick, follow the first three steps used for the frontside nose-slide to backside shove-it. Once you are familiar with the frontside noseslide, this trick will be far easier than you would expect.
2. Once in the frontside noseslide position, lift upward with your back foot while at the same time pushing forward with your front foot until you feel the front truck begin to grind on the top of the curb.
3. Grind backward for as long as possible.
4. When you want to come off, push downward with the back foot and away from the curb with your front foot until you know that all four wheels are on the ground and you are rolling backward.

VARIATIONS: Noseslide to crooked grind, half-Cab noseslide (backside and frontside), opposite-footed noseslide, noseslide to backward grind (frontside and backside).

BIG SPIN TO PIVOT TO REVERT

1. Roll up the transition with enough speed to do an axle stall or pivot.
2. Right before you get to the coping, do a big spin (360 backside shove-it) and land in a backside pivot.
3. After you land the pivot, keep rotating your body so that when you come into the ramp, you do a backside revert and ride down the wall backward.

VARIATIONS: Big spin, big spin kickflip, opposite-footed big spin.

Noseblunt

The noseblunt was invented by Mark Gonzales, and it wasn't until a few years later that other skaters began mastering the difficult maneuver.

BASIC NOSEBLUNT SLIDE

1. Ride parallel to the curb at whatever speed you want (probably slowly at first).

Chris Pastras executes the noseblunt slide.

2. Ollie toward the curb as if you were going to do a frontside lipslide but get more on top so that the nose of your board is over the edge of the curb instead of the rails.

3. Push down on the nose with your front foot so that the nose is sliding on top of the curb.

4. Stay on top of the slide.

5. When you want to come off, suck up on your back leg and push downward on the nose while staying directly above your board.

ALLEY-OOP NOSEBLUNT

1. Ride up the transition backside and when you are almost at the lip, ollie and turn your shoulders and body in the opposite direction (frontside alley-oop).

2. While in the air, stay directly above the board.

3. Point the nose down toward the lip and land in the noseblunt position.

4. As soon as the nose hits, push down with your front foot and at the same time bring your rear leg in toward your body (this action should let the front wheels clear the lip).

5. Lean forward and keep your rear leg sucked up until you know your rear wheels have cleared the lip. Once you know that you are clear, set the rear wheels down and ride away.

BLUNT SLIDE TO NOSEBLUNT SLIDE TRANSFER

1. Find a curb that's double-sided and fairly wide.

Eric Hoston executing a shove-it noseblunt slide to fakie.

2. Ride up parallel to the face of the curb and ollie frontside about forty-five degrees so that the nose of your board is facing upward and the tail is pushed into the curb (blunt slide).

3. Keep your weight centered slightly behind the board so that you slide, but the further you slide the more on top of the board you want to get.

4. When you start to feel a loss of speed, shift your weight to the opposite side of the curb and push down on the nose of your board until it gets into the noseblunt slide position.

5. When you want to come off, push forward on the nose and suck up the tail until the front truck clears the top of the curb.

VARIATIONS: Noseblunt slide to kickflip off, backside noseblunt slide, nollie noseblunt slide, fakie noseblunt slide.

Backward Front Truck Grinds

(BENCHES, CURBS, HANDRAILS, RAMPS)

Another trick that has gained popularity in the last few years is the backward front truck grind. Originally, this trick was done mostly on ramps and was called the "chink-chink" (I'm almost positive that Tony Hawk was the first to do it, but don't take my word for it); now it is a most common trick in the street because it feels good and has so many different variations.

FRONTSIDE 180 TO BACKWARD FRONT TRUCK GAZELLE OFF

1. Ride parallel toward the curb at whatever speed you want.
2. Do a frontside 180 ollie.
3. Land the front truck on the top of the curb (the tail of your board will be out in front), lean back, and grind backward for as long as you can.

Scott Sorenson executes the blunt slide to noseblunt slide transfer.

4. When you feel the need to come off the curb, take the weight off your front foot and shift it to your back foot until your back wheels are on the ground.

5. Now turn your body 180 degrees in the frontside direction (gazelle) until you are going forward.

FAKIE OLLIE TO BACKWARD FRONT TRUCK GRIND TO NOSESLIDE

1. Ride backward toward the bench or curb and pop a fakie ollie.

2. When you know that your front truck is over the top of the curb, set it down (but keep the tail of the board lifted) and start the backward grind.

3. Rotate your body backside and keep pushing down on the nose until you feel that you are now sliding on the nose of your board.

4. Slide for a little bit and then rotate your body about forty-five degrees (taking the weight off your front foot and shifting it to the back foot) until all four wheels are on the ground and you are riding away.

VARIATIONS: Frontside and backside 180 to backward front truck grind, frontside and backside 180 to backward front truck grind to fakie, fakie to backward front truck grind, fakie to backward front truck grind to crooked grind, frontside 180 to backward front truck grind to crooked grind.

Chris Miller doing a backside blunt slide.

RAMP TRICKS

Frontside Tailgrab

1. Ride up the transition at a slight angle, and when you are near the lip pop a frontside ollie.
2. Once you are in the air you'll want to suck up your back leg a bit farther then normal, reach for the tail with your trailing hand (left hand for goofy footers and right hand for regular footers), and grab it.
3. Keep turning just as you would for a regular frontside ollie.
4. Right before you clear the lip let go of the tail.
5. After you are under the lip set your wheels down, maintain your balance, and ride down the transition.

VARIATIONS: Backside tailgrab, tailgrab to fakie, fakie ollie tailgrab, frontside and backside tailgrab to tail smack, Caballerial tailgrab.

Front Truck Grind

1. Ride up the wall at an angle with enough speed to reach the lip (maybe more).
2. About four feet (1.2m) under the lip, do a frontside ollie up toward the coping.
3. Aim your front truck toward the coping with your front foot until you feel it grind but keep the tail of your board in the air.
4. Stay directly over the board throughout the grind and don't overturn (unless you want to do a revert).
5. When you want to come out of the grind, unweight your front foot a little and lean down the transition until you're not grinding anymore.

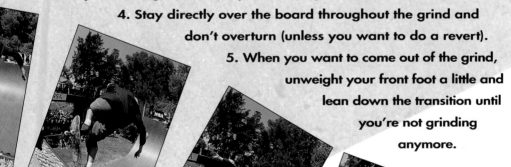

Remy Stratton does a no-handed
front truck grind at Kelly Belmar's pool.

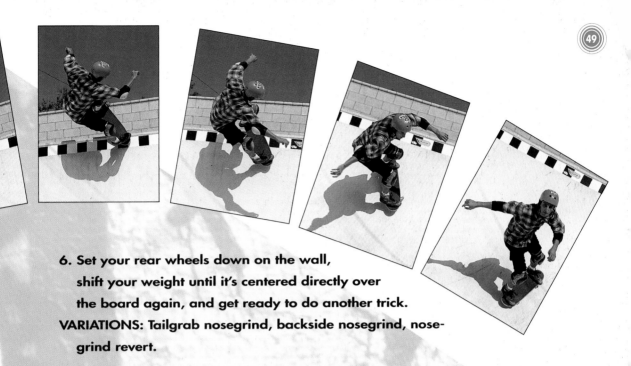

6. Set your rear wheels down on the wall,
   shift your weight until it's centered directly over
   the board again, and get ready to do another trick.
   VARIATIONS: Tailgrab nosegrind, backside nosegrind, nosegrind revert.

Backside Noseblunt Revert

1. Ride up the transition as though you were going to do a backside
   disaster (doing a 180-degree backside turn and landing in the
   middle of the board on the coping).
2. At the lip do a backside 180 (just like a disaster) but get your
   board high enough so that the nose is above the coping.
3. Push down on the nose until it lands in a backside noseblunt and
   sit on it for a second.
4. Push forward on the nose and suck the tail of your board up toward
   your body until you feel the front wheels clear the lip, while at the
   same time rotating your body backside another 180 degrees (revert).
5. Land backward, maintain balance, and ride down the transition
   backward.
VARIATIONS: Backside and frontside noseblunt, backside and
   frontside noseblunt slides, fakie noseblunt, fakie noseblunt to
   kickflip in, Caballerial to backside noseblunt.

Caballero Late Shove-it

1. Learn fakie 360 ollies (Caballerials) and late shove-its before
   trying this combination.
2. Ride up the transition backward; when you are near the lip, start
   rotation backside and suck your legs up into your body until the
   board is off the wall.
3. When you have reached the halfway point (180 degrees), do a
   backside shove-it but make sure your body stays over the board
   and keeps rotating through the 360.

4. Once the board has done the 180 shove-it and you have completed the fakie 360 ollie, land on the griptape side of the deck and ride down the transition.

VARIATIONS: Backside and frontside late shove-it, late shove-it disaster.

Body Varial Disaster

1. Ride toward the lip and grab like a regular mute air (grab the inside rail in front of your front foot with your forward hand).

2. As soon as you are above the lip, lift both feet off the board and turn your body 180 degrees but don't turn the board.

3. When your body has done the 180 (you are still holding the board with your mute hand), put your feet back on so that you are now doing a backside melon air.

4. You should now be directly over the coping.

5. Let go of the board and land the rails on the coping.

6. Quickly push down on the nose and suck your back leg upward and lean forward into the ramp, thus causing your back wheels to clear the coping (disaster).

7. Ride down the transition.

VARIATION: Indy body varial.

Chris Livingston executes a
backside body varial disaster.

Tom Boyle "the Rock"
doing a nose bonk.

Building Ramps

Text by Tim Payne

My name is Tim Payne, and there is a pretty good chance that I have built a ramp or skateboard park near or in your town. I've been to Europe sixteen times to build parks or ramps for skate contests and have worked with the N.S.A. (National Skateboarding Association) designing and building for quite some time. In the following pages, I am going to give you directions for building five different types of ramps for your own personal use (these ramps all exist at the Badlands Skatepark in Altamonte, Florida).

When starting any building project, first plan it out mentally from beginning to end. If you don't know how to use certain tools, be sure to ask someone to help you.

The first thing you need to consider is how to nail or screw your structures together. When nailing two-by-fours to a radius, or transition, use two 12d common nails or two 2½-inch (6.4cm) wood screws. When applying plywood, use 8d common nails or 2-inch (5cm) wood screws. To attach Masonite (this is optional and is used for a surface material only) or pipe, use 3-inch (7.6cm) dry-wall screws. (Mounting the pipe is discussed in the quarterpipe section.)

Quarterpipe

A good quarterpipe is always a necessity. This one would be good for learning technical lip tricks; it is small and easy to move so that you can place it at the end of the driveway or wherever else you'd like to put it.

MATERIALS NEEDED:
1 sheet ¾-inch (19mm) plywood
3 8-foot (2.44m) two-by-sixes
10 8-foot (2.44m) two-by-fours
8 feet (2.44m) black steel pipe (2 inches [5cm] in diameter)
4 sheets ½-inch (13mm) plywood
2 sheets ¼-inch (6mm) Masonite
1 sheet 12-gauge sheet metal, 8 feet (2.44m) long by
    16 inches (40.6cm) wide

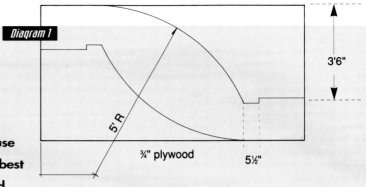

Diagram 1

5' R

¾" plywood

5½"

3'6"

If you're building the ramp outdoors, it is best to use pressure-treated wood. The best radius (from now on referred to as transition) I've found is 60 inches (1.52m) cut off at 42 inches (1.07m) tall. Take your ¾-inch (19mm) plywood and mark out the transition you prefer (diagram 1).

I'm sure you noticed the funny notch I put at the top of the diagram.

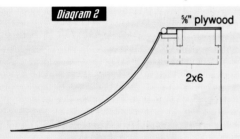

Diagram 2

⅝" plywood

2x6

This notch is to allow for the type of lip you want on your ramp. If you choose to have a deck (diagrams 3A and 3B), this will be the type of notch you'll use, which will allow you to attach your deck. Now it's time to mount the pipe. Drill 3 holes evenly spaced out in each pipe—⅜-inch (10mm) holes on top and ³/₁₆-inch (5mm) holes on the bottom. Mount the pipe with 3-inch (7.6cm) screws angling toward each other so they pull the pipes down together.

MATERIALS NEEDED FOR A 4-FOOT (1.22M) DECK:

1 sheet ⅝-inch (16mm) plywood
1 8-foot (2.44m) two-by-four
4 8-foot (2.44m) two-by-sixes

For a small deck without the extra expense (diagram 2), use only the original materials list. But for a 4-foot (1.22m) deck (diagrams 3A and 3B), you will also need the materials in the above list. After you have cut your transitions on the ¾-inch (19mm) plywood, measure 8-inch (20.3cm) center marks starting from the top for your two-by-fours.

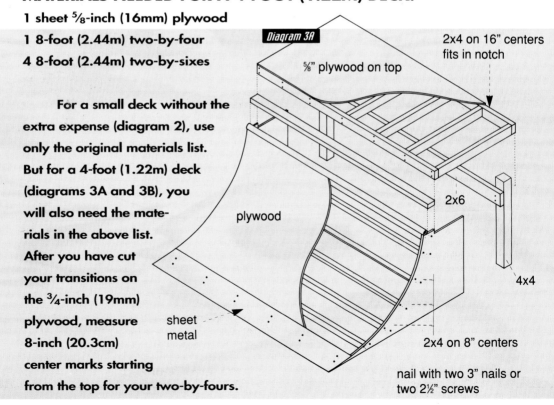

Diagram 3A

2x4 on 16" centers fits in notch

⅝" plywood on top

2x6

plywood

4x4

sheet metal

2x4 on 8" centers

nail with two 3" nails or two 2½" screws

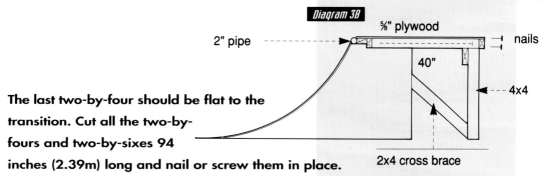

Diagram 3B

2" pipe — ⅝" plywood — nails

40"

4x4

2x4 cross brace

The last two-by-four should be flat to the transition. Cut all the two-by-fours and two-by-sixes 94 inches (2.39m) long and nail or screw them in place.

For the first layer of ½-inch (13mm) plywood, work from the top down. Cut the bottom piece of this first layer when you reach the ground. For the second layer, start nailing plywood from the bottom up. You'll have to slide the bottom piece of the second layer down a couple of inches (centimeters) so that its end touches the ground. Cut off the excess when you reach the top. By sliding the second layer down a couple of inches, the first and second layer seams won't meet—the ramp would be weak if the seams were in the same place. Nail or screw down all the plywood.

Now I bet you are wondering what that sheet of metal is for. I like to use this on the bottom to make it smoother and to keep the bottom of the ramp from tearing up. This alone will make your ramp last much longer. Drill and countersink 6 holes along the top and 6 more 4 inches (10.2cm) down, and screw the metal in place with a shim under it (diagram 4). For Masonite, use a ⅛-inch (3mm) shim; for a plywood surface, use a ⅜-inch (10mm) shim.

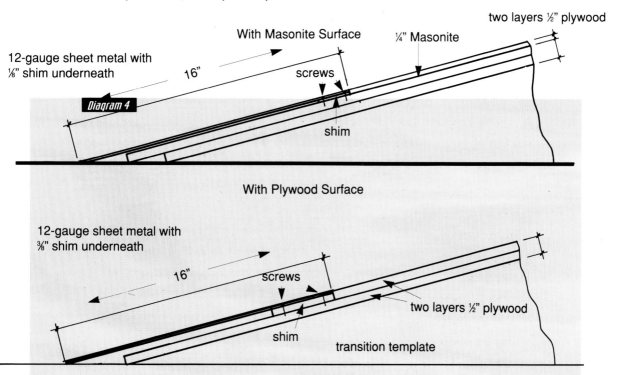

With Masonite Surface

¼" Masonite

two layers ½" plywood

12-gauge sheet metal with ⅛" shim underneath

16"

screws

Diagram 4

shim

With Plywood Surface

12-gauge sheet metal with ⅜" shim underneath

16"

screws

two layers ½" plywood

shim

transition template

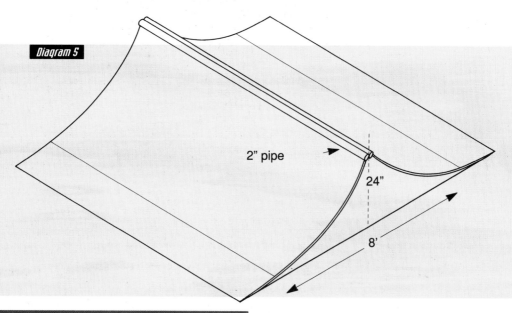

Diagram 5

2" pipe

24"

8'

Mini-Spine Ramp

MATERIALS NEEDED:

17 8-foot (2.44m) two-by-fours

1 sheet ³⁄₄-inch (19mm) plywood

8 sheets ¹⁄₂-inch (13mm) plywood

3 sheets ¹⁄₄-inch (6mm) Masonite

2 sheets 12-gauge sheet metal, 8 feet (2.44m) long by
   16 inches (40.6cm) wide

2 8-foot (2.44m) pieces pipe (2 inches [5cm] in diameter)

To make mini-spine ramp (diagram 5), start by laying out the transition on your ³⁄₄-inch (19mm) plywood (diagram 6). After you have cut out the transition, cut all the two-by-fours 94 inches (2.39m) long. Nail or screw together 2 two-by-fours at the top of your transition (diagram 7). Lay out marks for two-by-fours on 8-inch (20.3cm) centers starting from the top and working down. Now nail or screw two-by-fours to templates (made from ³⁄₄-inch [19mm] plywood) with the last two-by-four flat. Mount the pipe with 3-inch (7.6cm) screws (see the quaterpipe section for more detail). Finish your spine ramp with plywood, metal, and Masonite as described in the quarterpipe section.

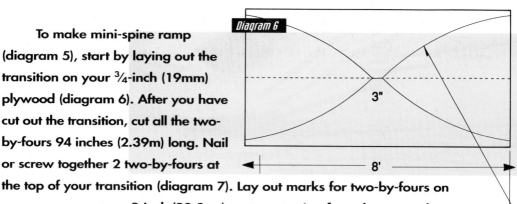

Diagram 6

3"

8'

Diagram 7

direction of screw

³⁄₈" top hole

³⁄₁₆" bottom hole
3" screw

2x4

2x4

Eric Nash doing an extremely high disaster.

Diagram 8

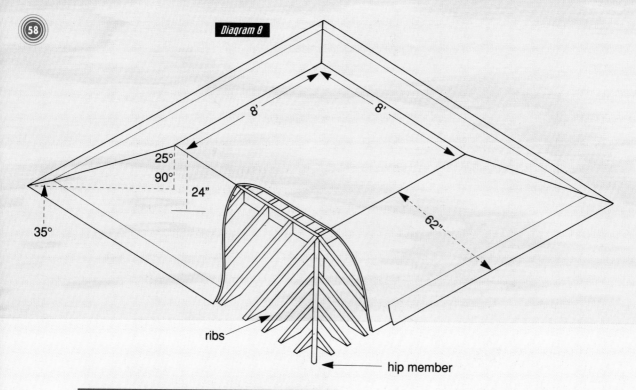

ribs

hip member

Pyramid Ramp

Next we have the pyramid ramp. A large area is required to build a
pyramid ramp, but if space demands, you can build just half of it.

MATERIALS NEEDED:
25 8-foot (2.44m) two-by-sixes
18 10-foot (3.05m) two-by-sixes
25 sheets ½-inch (13mm) plywood
13 sheets ¼-inch (6mm) Masonite
10 sheets 12-gauge sheet metal, 10 feet (3.05m) long
    by 16 inches (40.6cm) wide

First build an 8-foot-square (2.44m square) box. Cut 7 two-by-
sixes 93 inches (2.36m) long. Nail 2 8-foot (2.44m) two-by-sixes
to them on 16-inch (40.6cm) centers. Then nail 4 24-inch (61cm) legs
on them with a two-by-six ledger. Now turn the box over so it's
standing upright.

A good ramp angle is 25 degrees. So if you approve, cut 28 two-
by-sixes 62 inches (1.57m) long—you can get two of them out of the
10-foot (3.05m) two-by-sixes if you cut the first piece, flip it over, and
use it as a pattern for the second piece. Nail the 62-inch (1.57m) pieces
on 16-inch (40.6cm) centers so the assembly looks like diagram 8.

Now you need to fill in your hips. Use a string line to run
across the bottom of the ribs to get the outside point.

Next, cut the 4 hip members (it will help if you have a speed square to make the next angles). Now finish laying out each hip and fill in the shorter ribs on 16-inch (40.6cm) centers.

If you want some transition on the bottom (which is a good idea in most cases), add a ¾-inch (19mm) piece of plywood, cut 4 inches (10.2cm) wide and the length of the hip, across the bottom so your plywood rounds out, thus making a transition.

Starting with plywood at the top, work your way down; start your second layer from the bottom up. Finish with plywood, metal, and Masonite as described in the quarterpipe section.

Basic Rail Slide

I like long rail slides, so the one described is 20 feet (6.1m) long (diagram 9).

MATERIALS NEEDED:

2 20-foot (6.1m) two-by-eights
1 20-foot (6.1m) two-by-four
2 20-foot (6.1m) pieces black metal pipe,
   2 inches (5cm) in diameter
20 feet (6.1m) ⅜-inch (10mm) plywood,
   4 inches (10.2cm) wide
1 sheet ¾-inch (19mm) plywood, 4 feet
   (1.2m) long by 4 feet (1.2m) wide

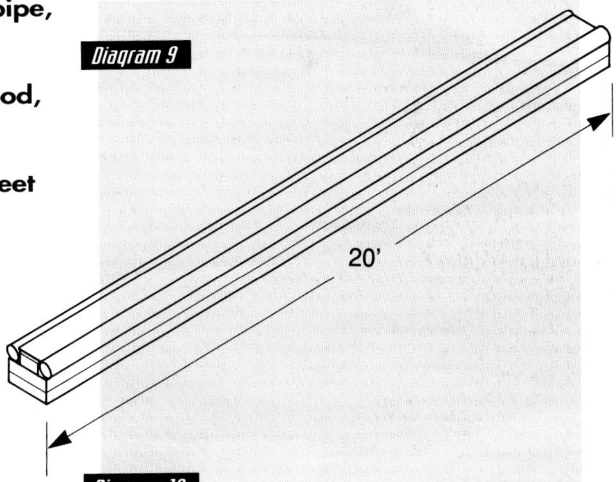

It is not necessary to make your rail slide as long as this, and you can always make it taller by adding on to the bottom. To get started, nail the two-by-eights together, then nail the two-by-four on top of them in the middle. Drill 5 holes in each piece of pipe (drill the same way as explained in the quarter-pipe section), and fasten them with 3-inch (7.6cm) drywall screws (diagram 10). Cut the ¾-inch (19mm) plywood on an angle to fit snugly against the pipe.

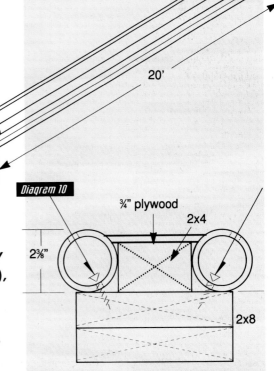

Diagram 9

20'

Diagram 10

¾" plywood

2x4

2⅜"

2x8

Hump Ramp with Rail Slide

These instructions are for 2 8-foot-wide (2.44m) hump ramps with a rail slide built in the middle (diagram 11). The middle rail slide is fun and also a challenging obstacle. The hump is 24 inches (61cm) tall, while the rail slide is 32 inches (81.3cm) tall.

MATERIALS NEEDED:

45 8-foot (2.44m) two-by-fours

22 sheets ½-inch (13mm) plywood

2 20-foot (6.1m) pieces black steel pipe

8 sheets Masonite

2 sheets 12-gauge sheet metal, 8 feet (2.44m) long by 16 inches (40.6cm) wide

2 sheets ¾-inch (19mm) plywood

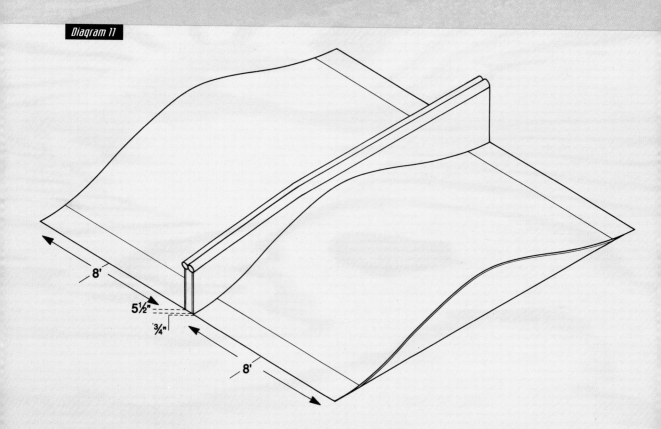

Diagram 11

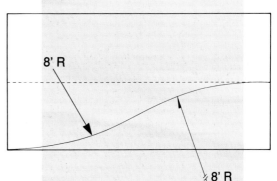

Diagram 12

Cut the ¾-inch (19mm) plywood pieces in half so each is 2 feet (61cm) by 8 feet (2.44m). Put an 8-foot (2.44m) transition on the bottom and top (diagram 12). Lay out the transitions on 8-inch (20.3cm) centers and nail together both humps with two-by-fours cut 94 inches (2.39m) long. Now build a box 16 feet (4.88m) long by 29 inches (73.7cm) tall on 16-inch (40.6cm) centers. Then nail plywood on both sides. This is for the rail slide. You can build it straight or with a slight incline of whatever degree you think would be challenging (diagram 13). It would probably be a good idea to use a large angle at first and as you get it wired, make the angle steeper to suit your skating.

Now stand the box up and slide the humps until they butt up against the side. Begin plying the hump, starting from the bottom and working your way up and over to the other side. Start the second layer from the opposite side and then finish with plywood, metal, and Masonite as described in the quarterpipe section, if desired.

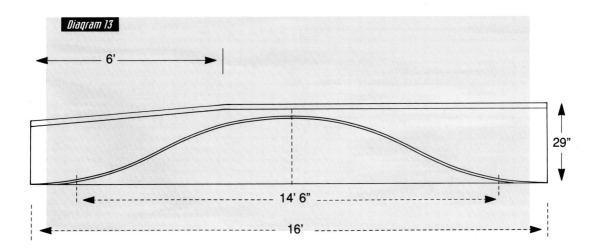

Diagram 13

Jordan Richter clutching a melanchollie to fakie and looking darn stylish to boot.

Skate-wear

Sometimes the most obvious idea slips right by without a second thought, so let's overstate the obvious, shall we? Comfort and function come way before fashion. That's simple enough, don't you think? For some reason, people not directly involved in skateboarding (i.e., people not in contact with it every day), and even some people who are, seem to think that there is actually clothing made specifically for skateboarding, and that it's very important to wear only this type of clothing while riding a skateboard. This is both very true and very false.

As stated before, skateboarding is a highly individualized activity. Ideally, people wanting to skateboard won't feel that in order to participate, they need to go to their local skate shop and buy the newest acceptable fashions. Unfortunately, just as in surfing, running, Rollerblading™, fencing, and other marketable activities, this isn't always the case, and some feel compelled to cling to some preset image, and exchange all their money for anything that makes them feel like they are part of a not-so-elite group. This is bad, very bad.

It's true that some clothes are better for skateboarding than others, just as some clothes are better for subarctic temperatures than others. You'd think this would be more than obvious, but sure enough, you'll find under-covered fashion victims sacrificing themselves for that drop-dead look straight through the winter months. If you feel compelled to skate in tight-fitting, man-made fabrics, more power to you. You are obviously on a much higher level than the rest of us. But you'd probably feel a lot nicer in a pair of loose-fitting pants or shorts, and a T-shirt.

Yes, it's true, many skatewear and other clothing companies will be the first to boast of the most comfortable, best-fitting clothing ever made. That's their business—to make their product seem better than the next guy's. And many manufacturers do make just that—good, well-made, well-designed, rugged clothing. If you have the means, I suggest you try on what looks cool to you and buy as much as you can afford. But if there is no way possible to get your hands on a few of these fine-tailored items, there are some things you can do to fight the war on funds.

DISCOUNT AND THRIFT STORES

Most every large town has a thrift store or discount store. Discount stores are either really huge, and buy in mind-numbing volume, in order to pass on the savings to the consumer, or buy seconds and slightly blemished items directly from the manufacturer. This means cheap clothes. These are also ideal places to look for good inexpensive shoes, lame sunglasses, and pretty much anything you need, plus they are probably one of the best arenas for playing hide-and-seek in existence today.

Thrift stores are cheaper than discount stores. That's because most of the items in these stores have been used before by someone and then discarded. Garage sales also qualify. This is where you

Frank Hirata in his typical skateboarding attire.

cash in on the generosity of others. Things that can be found in abundance at thrift stores are pants, coats, and jackets. If you're lucky you can find pants from the right era and they will be baggy and constructed fairly well. If not, buy them too big and take them in at the waist. Thrift stores are also excellent places to find bike parts, old records, 8-track tapes, and many other classic items. By all means, though (unless totally necessary), shy away from buying socks, underwear, or anything marked "soiled." This can only lead to bad.

MAKE YOUR OWN

This is how they did it on *Little House on the Prairie*. Look around your house for a sewing machine. If you don't find one, ask your mom — she probably gave up on the thing years ago and has stashed it somewhere far away. If you fail at home, butter-up the home economics teacher at your school and con him/her into giving you some time on the taxpayers' sewing machines. You'll also need a pattern. Go to a pattern or fabric store and ask for help. Tell them you want a pattern for baggy pants. If they don't have one, get a normal pattern, but buy an extra-large size. Shorts can be made by not using as much fabric as pants. Experiment. It will be hard at first, but after a while you'll get it wired just like anything else. Thrift stores are also an excellent place to find many yards of cheap fabric. Curtains and blankets work, too.

GET SPONSORED

This is a last resort. If you are good enough at skateboarding, you will get sponsored. But don't worry about it. Skateboarding is not about getting sponsored, it's about freedom, individuality, and fun.

If you are good enough to get a sponsor,

Frank Hirata again.

the company will most likely give you T-shirts. It's free advertising for them and it makes you happy in the process. Nowadays, many companies make shorts, pants, and other stuff. If not, your sponsor may be able to hook you up with other clothing or shoe sponsors who, when they recognize your skateboarding ability, will flow you some free products. DO NOT TRY TO GET SPONSORED JUST BECAUSE YOU WANT FREE CLOTHES OR ANY FREE PRODUCT. If you are deserving of anything, it will come to you. Be patient.

AVOID SKIN HOLES

You'll need shoes, too. Skating barefoot, although tragically cool, can actually be very painful. Shoes are a necessity. If you are planning to skateboard, you should probably get some. Would you like a few suggestions? Okay, read on.

High-top shoes are the preferred footwear for the discerning skateboarder, although there's nothing wrong with low-tops. High-tops usually offer a considerably larger amount of ankle support than their shorter counterparts. Since ankle injuries are one of the more common skate-related disasters, it would stand to reason that any extra precautions you can take will be greatly appreciated by the ball-and-socket joint that connects your foot bone to your leg bone.

The contact between one's feet and one's skateboard is very important. The closer you feel to your board, the more intimate your relationship will be. Many skateboarders will only wear thin-soled shoes to achieve extra feeling between their soul and their deck—so to speak. Others, including many larger others, need a bit of additional "cushion for the pushin'." Slightly more shock absorbent, but still soft-soled shoes are the choice of harder-stepping skateboarders.

Then there's the question of leather vs. canvas. Canvas is much softer and offers quick break-in time. Unfortunately, the price you pay for canvas' immediate gratification is coupled with its speedy path down the road of age. Not age in the sense of years—just the opposite, as a matter of fact. Age in the sense of wear. A canvas wearer might say something like the following: "Darn the luck. These shoes sure got old fast." Canvas does offer a friendly alternative for those socially aware consumers among us. It's not the skin of an animal—it's woven cotton and more-or-less environmentally safe.

Suede is also fairly easy to break in. A soft, brushed form of leather, suede makes its way down the path of age at a slightly slower pace than canvas, but it still feels the drag of grip tape, concrete, and masonite fairly terminally. When it feels that stuff, it breaks down, and that is where holes come from. Holes in your shoes lead to holes in your socks; holes in your socks lead to holes in your skin. Skin holes should be avoided at all costs.

Leather is the most rugged of the three materials. A pair of leather shoes should last considerably longer than their soft colleagues. But what you gain in tough cowhide and a slower pace down the aforementioned path of age, you lose in break-in time and feeling. Leather shoes also cost slightly more than the non-leather kind, so you might want to make your decision based on that. Here's another thing to think about: Leather and suede are animal skin. Ouch, that has to hurt.

So that's the lowdown on skate clothing. If you thought this was going to be some cute little guide to fashion—what's hot, and what's not—you thought wrong. Sorry, Charley. That would be the easy way around writing this section, and it just wasn't meant to happen.

Everything functioning correctly. Can you even imagine Tony Hawk pulling this tail-grab nose grind for the sake of fashion? I didn't think so.

Skating against no one, Pete DiAntoni grinds high atop the capsule's extension at Milwaukee, Wisconsin's Turf Skatepark.

Contests

Concentration plays a pretty big role during skateboarding contests. Here we see Bucky Lasek popping a leading-man half cab during a more-than-serious East Coast event.

There's a lot to be said for skateboarding contests. There, that's a safe statement. Sometimes it's hard to get the mind going and it's just a little easier to start off with a nice safe statement, so there it is.

Okay, ready for some grave stuff on skateboard contests? "They are seriously the worst," is what I heard a guy say. But another guy said, "I think contests are cool." So, what's a person to think?

Well, there are many good aspects to contests, and just as many bad ones. It's easy to see the validity of both sides of the proverbial coin, so you'll understand if both views are portrayed here for you to read. Hope you don't get mad or anything.

CONTESTS ARE LAME

They are seriously the worst. I mean, what is skateboarding about, anyway? I'll tell you, it's about doing what you want to do, having fun, and not caring. Contests cancel all that stuff out.

Fun? Yeah right. First, you have to pay. Skateboarding is free. I'm never going to pay to skate, ever. Except when I buy a new board or something, then it's okay. But why should I pay to skate against anyone? That's another thing—you have to compete against someone. What does competing have to do with it? Nothing, that's what. See, this is why it's really lame. In order to get results from a contest, the people first pay, then compete with each other, then have to be judged by some other people. How can you judge skateboarding? It's like saying, "Well this guy is way better

Jason Lee jumping and grabbing during an arena-style obstacle contest.

than that guy because he has a good style and he's smooth." Or, "Oh yeah, he's so good. He can do the most difficult, technical tricks." How can you compare different kinds of skateboarding? In contests, people aren't even doing the same tricks, or using the same lines in the same sequence. How can you say who's best? Then you've got to take into account the fact that it's not fun. Nope, not one tiny bit. Since skateboarding is all about fun and having a good time, it doesn't make sense that people would want to do something not fun while riding a skateboard. Snake sessions, an unfamiliar ramp or street course, hardly any practice time, and what if your session is at 7:00 AM? That's the worst. It's hard enough to make a fist in the morning let alone skate 100 percent. Runs are about forty-five seconds to a minute long and if you make one little mistake in that short time you are judged as being not as good as Joe Shmoe, who just happened to stay on in his runs, because he skated the ramp a week straight before the contest and was totally used to it. Plus, his girlfriend was there with him rooting him on. How could you beat that? Contests are the stupidest thing ever!

CONTESTS ARE REALLY COOL

I don't see anything wrong with them at all, except that there aren't enough of them. Look, you get to see all those friends from

Todd Congelliere is an excellent contest skater.
One of the reasons why he is excellent is that he has a place to skate.
Here is Todd slapping down a sick stalefish disaster in his very own backyard scene.

other places that you haven't seen since the last contest. You get to talk about skateboarding with them—eat skateboarding, breathe skateboarding, and excrete skateboarding as much as you want. It's like heaven. You and all your friends doing your favorite thing in the world—having fun, riding your skateboards.

Another thing is the competition. Pure energy, pure excitement, and pure livin'. Can contests be all those things and still be pure? Sure, why not? I mean, exposing your soul to the world to be judged by your peers and then taking the physical challenge of trying to skate as well as you've ever skated in your life. Self-control and self-discipline. It's okay if you don't do well, there will be another contest and you'll have time to progress before then. And let's not forget progression, shall we? Progression is in the air at a skateboard contest. A large group of skateboarders trying their hardest to push it to the limit. Progression seems to just build on itself. A contest makes you want to skate better than you ever have, because everyone wants that—it's the vibe in the air. *Do good, do good, do good.* How could you want to avoid any contest?

Contests also give our sport legitimacy. How do you expect the rest of the world to take skateboarding seriously if you don't have competition? All great sports have competition. That's why they're called sports, dummy. Skateboarders are always complaining about being harassed and looked down upon just because they skateboard. Well, if we compete, people will start to see that we are serious, not just a bunch of kids rolling around in the streets causing trouble. We're athletes.

There. Those are two views on skateboard contests. You can choose your favorite or combine the two, whichever feels best.

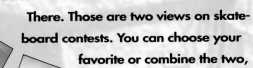

Holding a Contest

If you've ever thought of holding a contest, but thought it would be too much of a hassle, you were partly right. Contests are one of those things that make you ask yourself, "Why me?" But when it's all over you'll most likely be glad you went through all that trouble.

Holding a contest means dealing with all the organizational stuff, like getting a site to hold the contest, getting a ramp or obstacles, making sure the ramp or obstacles are quality and not junk (bad stuff to ride equals bad contest), advertising, getting judges, collecting fees, running heats, giving out prizes, babysitting the crowd of non-contest-skating skaters, and making sure peace and order are kept. It's really a lot easier than it sounds. Just follow these simple directions:

1. **DECIDE TO HAVE A CONTEST** Is that easy enough for you?
2. **CHOOSE WHAT KIND OF CONTEST YOU WANT TO HAVE**—street, miniramp, vertical, or freestyle. This is just slightly harder than number one and you could do number one in your sleep—literally. Judge the difficulty accordingly.
   STREET You'll need good obstacles and a place to put them. The place-to-put-them part is probably the hardest part of this whole list. If you can pull this off easily, you'll also be good at running a very large business or a small country. Public schools, local college campuses, shopping centers, or skateparks that already have the facilities to hold a street contest are some obvious locations. If you don't want to be that predictable, you can probably find other places to hold your little gathering. Pretty much anywhere flat, smooth, sparsely populated, and legal will work well. Illegal places work, too, but that's up to you. Just try not to get caught.
   VERT AND MINIRAMP This can be pretty tough, too. If you're into self-torture, you can always go the route of the school parking lot—just like the street contest, but you have to somehow build a ramp good enough and big enough to hold a contest in a fairly short time. This is hard. Ramps are big, heavy, expensive, and take some serious time and energy. Of course, you do get back what you give in a situation like this. Your contest will be both exciting to watch and skate in. The ramp audience isn't as spread out as the street, and it doesn't take up as much room as a street course. But not as many people can practice at

Ron Chatman. Contest-day melon to fakie over a pre-fab hip.

once and everyone will want to skate at the same time. Be patient. Set up practice heats and get someone big and mean to police them.

Skateparks or backyard ramps are ideal places to hold contests, too. The building problem is all but eliminated and the area is (hopefully) used to having skaters around. If it's in a backyard, be considerate to neighbors, and if it's at a skatepark, abide by the established rules.

FREESTYLE This is the easiest type of contest to pull off, aside from all the other contest hassles. All freestylers need is a large, level, smooth area. No obstacles. In freestyle it's important to make sure the judges are familiar with skateboarding. Freestyle is very technical and a lot of the maneuvers are too crazy for the untrained eye to figure out.

3. **GET PRIZES** Call up manufacturers, shops, local soft-drink bottlers, and anyone you think might be able to donate appropriate prizes. About prizes: The more the better. There are few things worse than doing well in a contest and having nothing to show for it. Unless you're one of those selfless competitors who just like competition for the sheer exhilaration of having your ability pitted against another's in a serious mental and physical battle. Liar.

Nautical enthusiast Mike Smith
yanking a frontside air above concrete sharpness.

4. **FIND JUDGES** Hurt skaters make good judges. This might sound brutal but at contests skaters get hurt. Heck, they get hurt everyday. There are always a few injured skaters wandering around at contests. Grab them. Make them judges, announcers, timers, or anything. Pay them a small fee, buy them lunch, give them a T-shirt, but make it worth their while. Judging is not fun, but someone has to do it and it might as well be someone who knows what's going on. Non-skater judges can be good, too. Girlfriends, boyfriends, parents, local charitable organization leaders, mayors, governors, teachers, coaches, etc. Just make sure they stay around the whole contest and don't play favorites.

5. **KEEP SCORE** It's hard to give judges specific things to look for during a contest, since individual skateboarders have individual approaches to skateboarding. A few buzz words you can use are consistency (number of falls), style, and difficulty. Judges eat those things up. The easiest way to score is on a scale of one to ten (like diving or something) or one to one hundred (like in school). Also mention to the judges that once a standard is set in their scoring, they should work around that standard. If the first skater you judge skated well and you gave him a high score, use that as a standard to judge the rest of the competitors. Judges must always be consistent.

6. **GET HOLD OF A P.A. SYSTEM (A GUITAR AMP WORKS PRETTY WELL) AND A MICROPHONE** You'll need everyone to hear the announcer, otherwise you'll have widespread anarchy.

7. **YOU'LL ALSO NEED MUSIC** A large portable stereo is ideal, but anything that plays music will do. Loud and fast is always a good choice.

8. **AGE GROUPS** are commonly used as a way to classify skaters, but you can have the skaters put themselves into groups by ability. You know, A (best), B (good), C (beginner). Warning: Good skaters might want to put themselves in an easier group than they belong in. Try to sort this out peacefully.

If done right, contests can be really fun events. Get through your first and you'll start thinking about the next one. Be sure to include skateboarders in your planning stages. They are the ones who will be skating in the contest and they will have a lot of ideas about how to do it. Listen to them.

chapter nine

Where to Get
Equipment

This is pretty simple, so it would stand to reason that it would be short, too. You know, short and simple. Everything you need to skateboard can be obtained one of two ways: from a skate shop or mail order.

If you live in a town with a relatively large population, a skate shop is just sitting there waiting to serve you. Look in the phone book under skateboards. It will more than likely tell you where the local skate shops are. If there are no stores that carry only skateboards, something listed under the skateboard heading should tell who carries skate equipment. Sporting goods stores, surf shops, and department stores sometimes recognize the need to bring the community quality skate products. If they are halfway reputable they will have all the pads (knee, elbow, wrist guards, and helmets), boards, wheels, trucks, and all the hardware you need to set up a quality board. If luck is on your side they might even have some good rugged clothing, to boot.

If you can't find anywhere to purchase what your heart desires, you have another avenue standing wide-open right in front of you—mail order. During skateboarding's shaky years, tons of mail-order companies came into existence and fed the skate-hungry locations not fortunate enough to have skate shops. Although you don't get to see what you're ordering, you have to pay for shipping, and then you have to wait for a few weeks, mail-order companies are known to have some really good deals compared to shops. If your area has a lack of an aforementioned skate headquarters, then mail order may be your only choice.

Natas Kaupas giving his deck a friendly tug.
He must be a really nice fella.

Carl Funk winging a melanchollie above a short flight of descending steps.

Setting up
a Board

There is no right or wrong way to set up a skateboard. If you buy your setup from a shop, ask them to put it together and watch how they do it. If that's impossible, go down to your parents' garage, get as many tools as you can find, and start on what looks easiest. Oh yeah, follow these directions, too:

Get all the materials you need to build a skateboard. How you acquire these items is up to you, but by all means get them all:

1 deck	8 mounting hardware nuts
2 trucks	grip tape
4 wheels	2 rails
8 sealed bearings	8 wood screws (for rails)
4 bearing spacers	2 riser pads
8 mounting hardware bolts	

You'll also need tools. Here's another list:

Sharp razor blade or X-acto™ knife
Steel file
Power drill
Socket adapter
½-inch socket (1.2 cm)
⅜-inch socket (10 mm)
⁹⁄₁₆-inch socket (14 mm)
⅛-inch allen key (3 mm)

If you don't have a drill, you can use a ratchet set for the nuts and a #2 Phillips head screwdriver for the screws.
If you don't have a ratchet set you can use an adjustable crescent wrench or pliers. Find or borrow these tools, otherwise you're going to have a hard time putting anything together.

STEP ONE: GRIP TAPE

1. Get enough tape to cover your board. Thirty-two inches (81 cm) should be plenty.
2. Peel the paper from the back of the tape.
3. Carefully place the tape on the board. Make sure the whole deck is covered.
4. Press the tape down hard so there are no air bubbles. A wheel on an axle can be used here, but your hand works just as well.
5. With a steel file, scrape the edge of the board so you'll have a guide line for cutting the excess tape.
6. With the X-acto™ knife follow the edge of the board and carefully cut off the excess tape.
7. File off the rough edges with the steel file, sit back, and breathe easy. Your tape is on and it looks really cool.

STEP TWO: PUTTING ON TRUCKS

1. Turn the board over and poke a nail or something small through the holes that have been predrilled in the board by the manufacturer.
2. Get the mounting hardware bolts and poke all eight of them through the holes in the top of the board.
3. Put the two riser pads on the bottom of the board. They have four holes in them and fit surprisingly well on the mounting bolts you just pushed through the deck.
4. Now put the trucks on the same way you did with the riser pads.
5. Find those eight mounting hardware nuts and put them on the exposed ends of the bolts—just finger tight, though.
6. Tighten the hardware with the ⅜-inch (10 mm) socket and a ⅛-inch (3 mm) allen key. If the bolts have a Phillips head instead of an allen head you'll need to use a Phillips head screwdriver. Call me crazy, but that's just how it is. Anyway, if you didn't notice, your trucks are on.

STEP THREE: PUTTING ON WHEELS

1. Find those bearings, spacers, and wheels you are supposed to have.
2. Take one bearing and slide it onto the axle of the truck.
3. Press the wheel onto the bearing really hard. This is how to insert the bearing into the wheel.
4. Take the wheel off the truck and put another bearing on the axle. You should also put a spacer on the axle.
5. Now press the side of the wheel that is empty onto the bearing and spacer. Press really hard. Make sure the bearings are sitting in the wheels straight and flush. If they're crooked your wheel won't spin right.
6. Place the axle nut on the axle and tighten with a ½-inch (1.27 cm) socket or a skate key. Don't make it too tight, though. The wheel should spin freely.
7. Now put the other three wheels on.

STEP FOUR: PUTTING ON RAILS

1. A power drill works best, but a Phillips head screwdriver works, too.
2. Place your rails where you think they look best.

3. Take a wood screw (included with the rails), insert it in the rail, and screw it into the board.
4. There, now your rails are on. Simple, huh?

You have just completed the assembly of your skateboard. Go ahead, take it for a ride. If you want, other plastic guards (like tail and nose protectors) can be attached to your board, but they aren't necessary. Ask your local skate shop employee for more information. Have some fun.

Jordan Richter steering a 180 ollie tail-grab over the hip at Mike McGill's Carlsbad Skatepark.

Safety

Equipment

There are really no set rules for safety when skateboarding. Aside from saying, "Try not to fall too hard," the only advice readily heard is, "Wear your pads." It does make sense, though. If you fall and hit a knee or an elbow or something, it would hurt less if you had that spot padded. There are all kinds of pads for all parts of the body. The most commonly used group includes knee pads, elbow pads, and a helmet. There are also hip pads, wrist guards, gloves, shin guards, and ankle and knee supports.

What you skate in is up to you, and most likely you will do what you want. But when you fall on your wrist without a wrist guard, or impact your knee without pads, you're going to wish you had your pads on. Here are some images of pads and where they go. Have a look see.

Knee supports or knee gaskets

Knee pads

Elbow pads

Wrist guards

Helmet

Fully protected boy

Ollie nose-blunt slide. Ed Templeton.

Hit the Road

If you are thinking about going to a skatepark and are also wondering where to find one of these beauties, look no further. Here's a long list of some of Earth's finest skate terrain. Some of the addresses are less than precise, but trust your luck and follow your nose and you'll find your way.

ARGENTINA
Piata Skatepark
Praia de Piata
Salvador, Buenos Aires,
Argentina

AUSTRALIA
The Skate Shed
1A / 25 Michlin St.
Moorooka QLD 4105
Australia
00 11 61 7 8921271

BELGIUM
Raes Skatepark
Moerstraat, 116
9230 Wetteren
Belgium

Roller Skating Dream
Slijpesteenweg, 24
8432 Leffinge-Middelkerke
Belgium
059 / 30 38 00

United Skates
Torhoutsesteenweg 90 f
Oostende
Belgium
059 / 50 30 53

BRAZIL
Abaeté
Clube de Campo Abaeté
Taubaté, São Paulo, Brazil

Academia Kickskate
Ave Nacoes Unidos, 1091
Novo Hamburgo, Brazil

Arpoador
Parque Garota de
Ipanema-Arpoador
Rio de Janeiro, Brazil

Barramares
Condominio Barramares-Barra
da Tijuca
Rio de Janeiro, Brazil

Dominio Skatepark
Rua Lucas Nogueira Garcez,
2940 Atibaia,
São Paulo, Brazil

Fox Skatepark
Rua Maria Candida, 1312
São Paulo, Brazil

Itaguara Country Club
Praca 13 de Maio, 90
Guaratingueta,
São Paulo, Brazil

Junior Skatepark
Rua Fernando Simonsen, s/n
São Caetano do Sul,
São Paulo, Brazil

Marina
Marina Barra Clube-Barra
da Tijuca
Rio de Janeiro, Brazil

Nautico
Clubo Nautico de Araraquara
Araraquara,
São Paulo, Brazil

Polato Skatepark
Ave Sete de Setembro, 1465
Guarulhos, São Paulo, Brazil

Polato Skatepark
Rua Schilling, 475
São Paulo, Brazil

Pontoes Da Barra
Barra da Tijuca
Rio de Janeiro, Brazil

Rampa Do Quadrado
Bairro da Urca
Rio de Janeiro, Brazil

Raticida Park
Ave Paes de Barros, 2694
São Paulo, Brazil

Riviera
Riviera del Fiori-Barra
da Tijuoa
Rio de Janeiro, Brazil

Santo André Skatepark
Ave Corrego do Cemitério, s/n
Santo André, São Paulo, Brazil

**São Bernardo Skatepark-
A.S.S.B.C.**
Ave Pereira Barreto, s/n
São Bernardo do Campo,
São Paulo, Brazil

Top Sport Skatepark
Rua Cardosa de Almeida, 80
São Paulo, Brazil

Turbo Jet Skatepark
Camboriu-SC
Brazil

Ultra Skate Center
Ave Morumbi, 8440
São Paulo, Brazil

ZN Skatepark
Ave Guaca, s/n
São Paulo, Brazil

CANADA
Century Skateboard Park
10533 123 St.
Edmonton, Alberta,
Canada T5N 1N9
(403) 482-1112

The Grassroots
12 Fisherman Dr.
Brampton, Ontario, Canada
(416) 480-5335

Langley Skate Ranch
20445 62nd Ave.
Langley, B.C.,
Canada V3A 5E6
(604) 534-3115

M and J's Skate Town
810 Rye St.
Peterborough, Ontario,
Canada K9J 6W9
(705) 745-7300

Off The Wall
1395 Ellice Ave.
Winnipeg, Manitoba,
Canada R3G 0G3
(204) 786-2418

Richmond Skate Ranch
7391 Elmbridge Way
Richmond, B.C.,
Canada V6E 1B8
(604) 273-7780

Spine and Grind Warehouse
32 Confederation Bay
Brandon, Manitoba,
Canada R7B 2T1
(204) 727-0986

Sports Afield II
310 Patillo Rd.
Tecumseh, Ontario,
Canada N8N 2L9
(519) 727-3967
(519) 727-6604

Torontosaurus Skatepark
3721 Chesswood Dr.
Downsview, Ontario,
Canada M3J 2P6
(416) 638-5047

Transition Skatepark
Donevan Rec. Complex
171 Harmony Rd.
Oshawa, Ontario,
Canada L1H 6T4
(416) 432-1577

DENMARK
Fabrikken Skatepark
Rudolfgårdsvej 13
8260 Viby J
Århus Denmark

Fælledparken Skatepark
Borgmester Jensens Vej
Nørrebro, Denmark

DOMINICAN REPUBLIC
World On Wheels
Winston Churchill Ave.
Santo Domingo,
Dominican Republic
(809) 565-3698

GERMANY
Berg Fidel Skatepark
Münster, Germany

Skatehouse
Max–Keith STR 25
4300 Essen–Sued
BRD–Germany

Jeff Pang clutching an ollie in the city that is a skatepark: New York.

JAPAN
Ascot Board Park
Osaka, Japan

MEXICO
Bony Skatepark
Hermosillo, Sonora, Mexico
Tel. 642-87

Club Bal-Skate
Ave. 4 Number 81
Mexico City, Mexico
(905) 558-2315

Coloso
Ave. Aldama
Ensenada, Baja California,
Mexico

Desastre
Ave. Morelos 1503
Toluca, Mexico
Tel. 790-58

Garra
Blvd. Estancia at Cerro
Ensenada, Baja California,
Mexico

Grand Prix
Papagayo Park
Acapulco, Mexico
Tel. 571-77

Heart Beat Club
Ave. San Luis Potosi corner
with Monterrey
Mexico City, Mexico
(905) 264-1945

Jungle Boy Skatepark
Tulum con Flamboyan
Smza. 23 L. 11-1 dep. 1
Cancun, Q. Roo, Mexico
Tel. 4-52-70

Mictlan
Ave. Hamm at Rio Fuerte
Mazatlan, Mexico

Parque Metalico
by Plaza del Angel
Guadalajara, Mexico
Tel. 215-585

Roller Condesa
Plaza Condesa
Acapulco, Mexico

Skate Paradise
Ave. Lomas Verdes
Bazar Perinorte
Naucalpan, Mexico

Skate Rock
Independencia 1580
Los Mochis, Sinaloa, Mexico
Tel. 502-63

Skate World
Culican, Sinaloa, Mexico

Skatopistas Del Sol
Ave. Lopez Mateos by Plaza
del Sol
Guadalajara, Mexico

Sport Plaza
Ave. Azueta at Constitucion
Mazatlan, Mexico

10½ Skatepark
Ave. Patria near Ave.
Americas
Guadalajara, Mexico

Tijuana Skatepark
Tijuana, Mexico
From border, ask cab driver to
take you to skatepark

Tiquius Skate and Surf
Calliende Ignacio
La Paz, Baja Sur, Mexico

Tropico Mini Ramp
Ave. Bangines at P. Loyola
Ensenada, Baja California,
Mexico

NETHERLANDS
Skatepark Van Nierup Sport
DR Phillipsplaan 25
6042CT Roermond
Netherlands

NORWAY
Rad Mini Park
Ostre Akerveien 91
Oslo 6, Norway

Session Skatepark
Bergen Mekaniske Verksted
Bergen, Norway

Session Skatepark
Stavanger, Norway

Skateout Skatepark
Hamang, Sandvika
Baerum, Norway

PERU
La Rampa Skatepark
Avenue Nicolas Arriala
Javier Prado Este
San Isidro, Lima 27, Peru

SINGAPORE
Rock 'N' Roll Skatepark
Block 21, #01-45
Flanders Square, Petain Rd.
Singapore 0820

SOUTH AFRICA
Aston Bay Ramp
Natal

Boogaloos Skatepark
Johannesburg

Legends Skatepark
Krugersdorp

Look Ahead Skatepark
Johannesburg

Parrow Skatepark
Cape Town

Pink Pipe Skatepark
Pretoria

Prichard Security Skatepark
Cape Town

Rox Skatepark
Natal

**Skateboard Warehouse
Skatepark**
Pretoria East

Surf News Skatepark
Natal

SPAIN
Las Arenas Skatepark (Algorta)
Pais Vasco, Spain

Barcelona Skatepark
Cataluña, Spain

La Cantera Skatepark (Algorta)
Pais Vasco, Spain

Duesto Skatepark (Bilbao)
Pais Vasco, Spain

Madrid Skatepark
Madrid, Spain
From Moncloa subway station,
take bus 83 to Carretera

Mini Ramp of Tapia
Asturias, Spain

Mini Skatepark of Avilés
Asturias, Spain

Puerta de Hierro Skatepark
Madrid, Spain

Ramp of Pontevedra
Galicia, Spain

Ramp of Zarauz
Pais Vasco, Spain

Skatepark of Malaga
Andalucia, Spain

Skatepark of Palma de Mayorca
Baleares, Spain

UNITED KINGDOM
Livingston Skate Park
Livingston, Scotland
United Kingdom

South Sea Skatepark
South Sea, England
United Kingdom

UNITED STATES

ALABAMA
Rampage Skatepark
501 Springville Cir.
Birmingham, Alabama 35215
(205) 854-9617

ARIZONA
Thrasherland
11748 W. Glendale Ave.
Glendale, Arizona 85307
(602) 872-9737

ARKANSAS
Bike Haus
111 Buena Vista
Hot Springs, Arkansas 71913
(501) 525-4500

Skatepark of Little Rock
Kanis Park, S.
Mississippi Ave.
Little Rock, Arkansas 72205
(501) 227-0599
(public park, free)

Skate Station
225 N. Gregg St.
Fayetteville, Arkansas 72701
(501) 442-6526

CALIFORNIA
Carlsbad Skatepark
On the corner of Palomar
Airport Rd. and Business
Park Dr., Carlsbad,
California 92008
(619) 598-8688

Lipslide
1509 Bonnie Beach Pl.
Los Angeles, California 90063
(213) 265-0412

Shasta County YMCA
1155 Court St.
Redding, California 96001
(916) 246-9622

Visalia YMCA
211 W. Tulare Ave.
Visalia, California 93277
(209) 627-0700

COLORADO
Fort Skate
105 E. Lincoln Ave.
Fort Collins, Colorado 80524
(303) 493-0943

Independent Skatepark
123 Rear East Bijou
Colorado Springs, Colorado
80903
(719) 630-8674

Jamaica Jim's Skatepark
3040 S. Platte River Dr.
Englewood, Colorado 80110
(303) 761-9317

CONNECTICUT
Connecticut Bike and Skate
86 South St.
Bristol, Connecticut 06010
(203) 582-3334

The Playground
35 Capitol Dr.
Wallingford, Connecticut
06492
(203) 269-3205

FLORIDA
Astro Skating Center
875 E. Cypress St.
Tarpon Springs, Florida 34689
(813) 938-5778

Bulldog Skatepark
741 Mayflower
Fort Walton Beach, Florida
32548
(704) 863-4500

Grinders Skatepark
4232 20th St. West
Bradenton, Florida 34205
(813) 751-4444

Island Skateboard Park
U.S. Hwy 41
Springhill, Florida 34610
(904) 799-5182

Kona Skatepark
8739 Kona Ave.
Jacksonville, Florida 32211
(904) 725-8770

Mike McGill's Indoor Skatepark
201 Douglas Ave.
Oldsmar, Florida 33614
(813) 855-2763

Ramp Age
1105 S. Division Ave.
Orlando, Florida 32805
(407) 872-1554

Skateboard Stadium World
3731 N.E. 36th Ave.
Ocala, Florida 32670
(904) 368-5088

Stone Edge Skateboard Park
1848 U.S. 1
South Daytona, Florida 32019
(904) 761-1123

GEORGIA
Skateboard Connection
472-D Flowing Wells Rd.
Martinez, Georgia 30907
(404) 855-1805

The Skateboard Warehouse
909-B Roosevelt Ave.
Albany, Georgia 31701
(912) 883-5823

Skate Zone
3602 Lawrenceville HWY
(HWY 29)
Tucker, Georgia 30084
(404) 491-0787

Surf's Up Streetwaves
6709 Tribble St.
Lithonia, Georgia 30058
(404) 482-7471

The Wall Skateboarding Park Inc.
2209 Mountain Terrace Rd.
Dalton, Georgia 30720
(404) 226-1333

HAWAII
Aala Park
280 N. Kings St.
Honolulu, Hawaii 96817
(808) 522-7022

Jungle Land Skatepark
Shaw St.
Lahaina, Maui, Hawaii
(808) 661-8443

Kailua Recreation Center
21 S. Kainalu Dr.
Kailua, Hawaii 96734
(808) 261-0680

Kalakaua Recreation Center
720 McNeill St.
Honolulu, Hawaii 96817
(808) 848-0514

ILLINOIS
Air Waves SK8 Park
2021 S.W. Washington St.
Peoria, Illinois 61650
(309) 672-1800

4 Wheels Out
2350 Hassell Rd.
Hoffman Estates, Illinois 60195
(708) 885-8170

Rotation Station
7915 N. Alpine Rd.
Rockford, Illinois 61111
(815) 654-7477

Skank Skates
1101 South Grand Ave. East
Springfield, Illinois 62703
(217) 522-7267

INDIANA
Edgewood Indoor Skateboard Facility
1220 W. Main St.
Greenfield, Indiana 46140
(317) 462-9889

Swinney Park Skateboard Center
Swinney Park
Fort Wayne, Indiana
(219) 422-1490

IOWA
Ollie In Outdoor Skatepark
Dubuque Sports Complex
Nightingale Ln.
Dubuque, Iowa 52001
(319) 582-7244

Rampage Indoor Skatepark
4004 W. Kimberly
Davenport, Iowa 52806
(319) 386-8762

KANSAS
Ally Oops Outdoor Skatepark
940 N. Wichita St.
Wichita, Kansas 67203
(316) 264-3541

Wild West Sk8 Park
9020 W. Harry
Wichita, Kansas 67213
(316) 722-0470

KENTUCKY
Audubon Skatepark
3310 S. Preston St.
Louisville, Kentucky 40213

**Green River Skateboard Inc.
(Skatepark)**
463 Spurlington Rd.
Campbellsville, Kentucky
42718
(502) 465-8667

Skate Club Skatepark
3320 Springford Ave.
Louisville, Kentucky 40206
(502) 895-4532

LOUISIANA
**Surf N Skate
Explorer Skatepark**
116 Guilbeau Rd.
Lafayette, Louisiana 70506
(318) 981-0976

MAINE
Ratz Skatepark
19 Landry St.
Biddeford, Maine 04005
(207) 284-1500

MARYLAND
Ocean Bowl Skatepark
3rd St. & St. Louis Ave.
Ocean City, Maryland 21842
(301) 289-BOWL

MASSACHUSETTS
Cross Skatepark
5 First St.
Southwick, Massachusetts
01077

Z.T. Maximus Motor Sports
324 Ridge Ave.
Cambridge, Massachusetts
02138
(617) 576-4723

MICHIGAN
K-Zoo Skate Zoo
1502 Ravine Rd.
Kalamazoo, Michigan 49007
(616) 345-9550

SK8 Escape
184 W. Wardion
Highland, Michigan 48031
(313) 887-0099

T.C. Skate (Great North Sports)
467 U.S. 31 South
Traverse City, Michigan 49684

Wind, Waves, & Wheels
198 Northland Dr.
Rockford, Michigan 49341
(616) 866-9584

MINNESOTA
Gregg Witt's Funhouse Ramps
301 E. Mark St.
Winona, Minnesota 55987
(507) 454-2494

Twin Cities Skate Oasis
1201 E. Lake St.
Minneapolis, Minnesota 55407

MISSISSIPPI
Oasis Surf And Skate
200 Pass Rd. STE #1
Gulfport, Mississippi 39507

Steve's Southcoast Skatepark
515 Krebs Ave.
Pascagoula, Mississippi 39567
(601) 769-2007

MISSOURI
Bullet Skateclub Inc.
505 W. 13th St.
Joplin, Missouri 64801
(417) 782-2886

Radz Skatepark
1300 St. Louis St.
Springfield, Missouri 65082
(417) 869-7237

Splash Skatepark
1755 Clarkson Sq.
Chesterfield, Missouri 63017
(314) 532-8085

NEBRASKA
Eat Concrete Skateboard Park
6101 Irvington Rd.
Omaha, Nebraska 68134
(402) 572-7676

Fast Ramp
300 N. Second St.
Lincoln, Nebraska
68508-2340
(402) 438-1210

NEW HAMPSHIRE
Zero Gravity Inc.
522 Amherst St.
Nashua, New Hampshire
03063
(603) 595-4250

NEW JERSEY
Jeff Jones Skatepark
516 East Bay Ave.
Manahawk, New Jersey
08050
(609) 597-5755

NEW YORK
Back Alley Skates
200 Main St.
Binghamton, New York 13905

Halfpipe Indoor Skate Park
612 Corporate Way
Valley Cottage, New York
10989
(914) 268-4084

**Saratoga Springs Skateboard
Park**
Corner of Lake Ave. and
Granger St.
Saratoga Springs, New York
12866
(518) 587-3550

*Gary Harris jumping an ollie in an urban skate.
Calgary, Alberta, Canada.*

Skateboard Madness
2466 Charles Ct.
Bellmore, New York 11710
(516) 679-5047
(516) 868-0100

**YMCA of Kingston and
Ulster County**
507 Broadway
Kingston, New York 12401
(914) 338-3810

NORTH CAROLINA
Eastern Vert Skatepark
2390 E. Sprague St.
Winston-Salem, North Carolina
27117
(919) 785-1889

**The Ramphouse Indoor
Skatepark**
220 Winner Ave.
Carolina Beach,
North Carolina 28428
(919) 458-3906

OHIO
Boarder's Edge Skate Shop
320 W. National Rd.
Englewood, Ohio 45322
(indoor mini ramp)
(513) 832-0000

Ohio Surf and Skate
1306 Wyoming St.
Dayton, Ohio 45410
(indoor mini ramp)
(513) 253-1119

Sunsports Skateboard Park
175 Fairway Blvd.
Whitehall, Ohio 43213
(614) 575-2929

Hi-Rollers
6217 Charlotte Ave.
Nashville, Tennessee 37209
(615) 356-0623

TEXAS
Island Skatepark
2501 Padre Blvd.
South Padre Island, Texas
78597

Jeff Phillips' Indoor Skatepark
2551 Lombardy Ln. #150
Dallas, Texas 75220
(214) 358-0052

Power Plant Skatepark
2309 Gardenia
Austin, Texas 78728
(512) 244-7774

Skatepark of Houston
4818 Orange Grove
Houston, Texas 77039
(713) 449-4438

Skatetime
2935 Bachman Dr.
Dallas, Texas 75220
(214) 350-8947

Y–Not Sk8 Warehouse
927 Crosstimbers Dr.
Houston, Texas 77022
(713) 694-9413

UTAH
Mrs. C's Skatepark
9139 S. 255 West
Sandy, Utah 84070
(801) 266-9518

VIRGINIA
Laurel Skatepark
Glen Allen, Virginia 23060
(804) 672-6273

Lynnhaven Park
Great Neck Rd. &
1st Colonial Rd.
Virginia Beach, Virginia
23456
(804) 422-5122

Mount Trashmore Park
South Blvd.& Edwin Dr.
Virginia Beach, Virginia
23456
(804) 490-0351

Red Wing Park
General Booth Blvd. &
Prosperity Rd.
Virginia Beach, Virginia
23456
(804) 481-4340

WASHINGTON
Air Radical Skate Park
111 N. 3rd Ave.
Yakima, Washington 98902
(509) 453-4008

WISCONSIN
Turf Skatepark
4267 W. Loomis Rd.
Greenfield, Wisconsin 53221
(414) 281-9000

OKLAHOMA
Daddy-O's Skate Emporium
6945 E. 38th St. #B
Tulsa, Oklahoma 74145
(918) 622-7471

PENNSYLVANIA
Cheap Skates II
13 Swartley Rd.
Line Lexington, Pennsylvania
18932 (indoor ramp)
(215) 997-2313

**The Chris Bernstine Memorial
Skatepark**
Fourth St., Elm Park
Williamsport, Pennsylvania
17701
(717) 327-8609

DJ's Indoor Skatepark
1414 Broadhead Rd.
Aliquippa Pennsylvania 15001
(412) 375-2099

Magic Skatepark
Rt. 562
Jacksonwald, Pennsylvania
19606
(215) 372-6624

PA Cheapskates
1064 3rd St.
North Versailles, Pennsylvania
15137
(412) 829-2728

Rip the Lip
110 Brimmer Ave.
New Holland, Pennsylvania
17557
(800) 525-5843

Shady Skates
7501 Penn Ave.
Pt. Breeze
Pittsburgh, Pennsylvania 15208
(412) 731-5400

RHODE ISLAND
Skatehut
7 Dike St.
Providence, Rhode Island
02909

Skater's Edge
334 Knight St., Bldg. 3
Warwick, Rhode Island 02886
(401) 732-1004

SOUTH CAROLINA
Charleston Hanger
7282 Spa Rd.
Charleston, South Carolina
29418
(803) 863-8612

**Transitions Indoor
Skateboard Park**
50-C Woods Lake Rd.
Greenville, South Carolina
29609
(803) 370-1945

TENNESSEE
Crown, Inc. Skateboard Park
HWY 41
Winchester, Tennessee 37398
(615) 962-0644

The Edge
5456 Pleasant View
Memphis, Tennessee 38134
(901) 377-0452

INDEX